The Art of Coaching High School Tennis

2nd edition

Copyright 2015 Bill Patton

ISBN: 1942597037

ISBN 13:9781942597032

Introduction

The chief aim of this book is to help you take high school tennis to the next level where you are. Also, USATennisCoach offers a high school coach certification that is based mainly on this book, so once you have read it through, you will be ready to achieve the first level of certification. I want to show different ways to make your team a better experience, making it more organized, more fun, etc. There is a movement taking place in high school tennis among those who want it to become a hot bed for player development at every level. The vast majority of players are the future adult players will spring from the ranks of high school players. A handful of very athletically talented freshmen, if identified early and developed properly could become professionals in 10 years time or less. For coaches, this book is a consultancy for thoughts about high quality coaching. For parents, it's an inside look at a tennis program from a coach's point of view. Finally, for players, there is section to help you see the bigger picture to help you decide if high school tennis is right for you. In less than 1% of cases high school tennis is not right for the player.

Consider this: What if coaches where were pressed into duty by the school were to reach out and collaborate with other tennis enthusiasts in the area? What if parents lobbied hard to have a highly skilled coach hired, and also did some fundraising to augment a salary to make the program worthwhile for the coach to give up other work? What if everyone worked together, coach, school, parents and players to make the high school tennis team the best experience that could happen at that school? It can happen. Then a high school team becomes a junior development program as it is in almost every other sport.

A disturbing trend in sports has continued in the last 10-15 years, where families have begun more and more to be consumers of a school simply for it's sports program. So the decision of where to go to school, and/or play for the team is based on 'what can it do for me?'. At it's worst, this problem shows up when the player has enrolled in school, transfers to another school, or even a third or fourth school in search of the greener grass of opportunity. This happens much more in football and basketball, but the same sort of consumer driven attitude can pervade the arena of high school tennis. Some elite players feel they need to decide whether to play high school tennis or not, in favor of more time with a private coach or program, it behooves the high school coach and athletic program to do all they can to make the program as attractive as possible. I never recommend bending to the will of a teenager, but you will see in this book anecdotes of dynamic decision making for the greater good. So, welcome to the complexity of high school tennis coaching!

Bill Patton 12/1/2015

Actually I think Art lies in both directions - the broad strokes, big picture but on the other hand the minute examination of the apparently mundane. Seeing the whole world in a grain of sand, that kind of thing. ~ Peter Hammil

Overview

You obviously want to be an effective high school tennis coach, so welcome aboard. You will receive many of the tools, and think through many of the problems of high school tennis, so you can fix them or avoid them altogether. Any feedback you give me via email is greatly appreciated, as this second edition is greatly influenced by comments from readers since it was first published. bill@pattonschooloftennis.com

We will cover the following:

- Where do high school tennis coaches fit with the school, athletic director (AD), and educational pecking order?

- Developing a coaching style from a management perspective

- Running meetings

- Planning a periodized schedule for any ability level of team

- Goal-setting for the team and individuals

- Key strategic principles for the high school player

- Adding a new tactic to your team's repertoire

- Conditioning on limited time

- Realistic stroke improvements in 10 weeks

- Managing injuries
- Adjusting your plan to fit the team
- Team unity
- Mental training for groups and individuals
- Game Day Mantra
- Dealing with problem players
- Develop leadership in team captains
- Time-saving tips, setting the tone
- Planning a schedule
- Observing energy level of your team
- Precious moments
- Showing anger or disappointment
- Post-season preparation
- Fun games, and activities, using stories to teach
- Celebrating the season and the players
- And Much MORE!

THE ART OF COACHING HIGH SCHOOL TENNIS 2ND EDITION

Bill Patton

Thank you Mom, for Understanding

CHAPTER ONE
Big Picture Planning - Team and School

To be a good citizen, it's important to be able to put yourself in other people's shoes and see the big picture. If everything you see is rooted in your own identity, that becomes difficult or impossible. ~ Eli Pariser

The most important factor that affects all future planning for you and your team is knowing the place of the coach in your school's educational pecking order. Schools vary widely in their support of sports and also in support of certain sports over others. In 26 seasons of coaching at the high school level, I have never come across an athletic director who has played tennis at a high level. They generally don't understand the game. Athletic directors may see tennis merely as an individual sport, and might not see how it can be played as a team game. They may also only see tennis as a thorn in their side, on the other hand they may recognize that it is a great outlet for the best and brightest students at the school. This simple fact of creating more student athletes can be very motivating to an athletic director. Some schools are so small, however you may face competition with other sports who do not want their athletes to crossover into tennis. There is a strong perception among athletic directors in my area that tennis coaches are not the strongest team players, and have higher expectations, demands, and desire special treatment ahead of other coaches, even though they are in a non-revenue-producing sport.

Here are some things I do to break this pattern.

1. Accept conditions as they are

2. Don't immediately ask for an increase in the budget

3. Do your own fundraising.

4. Encourage players on the team to engage the other athletes in school about their sport, and what kind of experience are they having, they may reciprocate

5. Attend at least one football and basketball game during the season

Without seeming as though you are going over the head of the athletic director, engage with other administrators at the school including the principal on an informal basis. The principal is more likely to have played tennis, and they will have a greater interest in talking about the high-performing students you have on your team. Engage the principal and brag about a kid or two, what they are learning on the tennis court, and how they represent the school.

School secretaries and custodians run the school, so be sure to befriend them. If you really want to get a glimpse behind the scenes, talk with students and parents about the true culture of the school. I have worked at schools where the kids run the school, and others where administrators attempt to rule the school with an iron fist.

There are often schools that have factions of people that have an agenda, that may run counter to what you want to achieve in your program. For example, militant, non-supportive teachers who schedule assignments in such a way that teams with early release from school will feel conflict over missing them.

Forging an understanding with the principal can help with that problem.

When schools have a culture coercive to sports, or particularly to tennis, athletic directors may opt not to find a truly qualified high school coach. They choose instead a teacher at the school to hold a clipboard, because there are fewer headaches involved, and they know they can control teacher who does not have tenure. There is an unwritten expectation that P.E. teachers will also coach teams, so if one is available, they will face pressure to do that within the athletics/physical education department. This can sometimes present an opportunity for an outside or assistant coach position for someone who is a tennis teaching professional.

Note to parents: The above information sheds light on why the school might not be excited about a top coach coming into the school, or why they don't want to have extra support in the form of a guest coach. Your situation can be very tenuous since school officials and athletic directors many times are bombarded with special requests and issues with coaches from parents. It is in your best interest to be as diplomatic as possible and prove yourself not to be just another complaining parent. Look for ways to support and empower the overall athletic program, the athletic director, and the coach and the school at large, and then you will find much more influence in having your voice heard. If you are unable to engage in the above, simple discourse with coach or athletic director is paramount. Respect the coach at all times! Be the parent who empowers people to make great decisions.

Note to the tennis professional who might want to coach a high school team hoping for access to the courts: A few issues you may assume would be easy to resolve but aren't easy or can be almost completely non-negotiable are:

1. Use of the courts to teach lessons, run a program or an event

2. Taking the players to a team tournament

3. Making a special trip to see pro or college tennis.

The main concerns of a school district is liability from the standpoint of injury, misconduct due to lack of supervision, and sometimes simply opening up another problem maintaining equal use. Sometimes, if you have insurance such as that offered by USPTA and PTR, or a high school tennis coaches association, then that is enough to cover the district as well. Here it is very important to use the chain of command by asking the AD, and then asking permission to talk to the principal. On one occasion, I even went to the business office of the district to gain permission to use the courts, and it was granted. It's best not to assume that you will be granted full access. In the end, the assistant superintendent of business services saw a reduced budget and a higher income stream and the rest is history. At other districts, supreme care of the facility means extremely limited access to anyone, no matter the potential financial benefit. Finally, issues in regard to school district unions, and rules concerning facility access and supervision can be a major problem in gaining use of the courts and bathrooms outside of school hours. So find your way, and make friends in the administration!

CHAPTER TWO

Big Picture Planning - The Whole Season

A big part of leadership is just being comfortable with the fact that some decisions really are only yours. ~ Helene D. Gale

It's a great idea to break down the season into pieces. I like four pieces, but the structure of your team's play could be much different. In our 10 to 15-week Northern California Season, I break it into the Pre-Season, First Half of Regular season, Second Half of Regular Season, and Post-Season. The pre-season is almost four weeks, each half of the regular season is three weeks, and the post- season is two weeks. For great teams that are in position to play deeply into the post season including the NorCal Regionals (the end of the road in California), the season can be 15 weeks long. Some of our Sections start one week earlier than other sections in the NorCal Region. Non-Championship teams may have 10 week seasons, and still some schools may not play during that entire time, some schools only really operate for 7 or 8 weeks. Whatever is true for you, maximize the amount of time, and make the best use of your time with a solid overall plan.

There are two mistakes that coaches make. 1. Conditioning through the entire season. Please don't wonder later why your team has nothing in the tank at the end. 2. Not conditioning extremely hard through a full four weeks, even at the expense of some pre-season diminished performances.

For many teams the best plan is to be prepared for late season and post season play. For other teams the only real goal is to prepare for the rivalry matches. When I look at my calendar, I set up a full four-week conditioning schedule, and then I look for two key regular season match ups. Once we have ended a really tough stretch in the season, I give the players a very easy fun day. I let them know they are facing a tough stretch, and no matter result of the matches, we will still have the fun day.

Sometimes I see my team might be getting a little flat or stiff, so I add in a short burst of conditioning, but I make sure that its at least 3 days prior to any difficult competition, and I like to include a nice long stretching routine to bring us back to what we developed in our training phase. My personal opinion is that once you develop flexibility, you don't lose it easily, but over time you will, so I do the major stretching routines during our pre-season, a little at the beginning of each practice, and then a major 30 one halfway through the season.

Often we get so complicated in our approach that we never measure if our players are actually become quicker. I decided to take the standards given for what is an average quickness score for a nationally ranked or young professional at 18 years of age, and I have my team strive to achieve that level. The goal was to have someone do the spider run in 15.4 seconds or lower. In 1999, I had two players who did under 16 seconds. My number one player did 15.4. In 2000, my goal was to have the entire varsity do under 16 seconds. I was amazed by what happened. One player did 14.9, a group of players did 15.1 and 15.2, and 9 players total were under 16 seconds. Our legs had become weapons. Our opponents found that shots that were winners against other teams came back one more time as most every player on the team was capable of running down a lot of difficult shots. We were able to put a tremendous amount of pressure on other teams by making it very difficult to win a point. We won what I consider to be our 'miracle' championship that year. But really through hard work these players who were not incredibly physically talented had become much better athletes and created their own luck.

An anecdote from the 1998 season shows the importance of working on conditioning and court speed. At midseason the top 2 players in league faced off with the top player from another school very motivated to beat my top player and overtake him as the favorite to win the league title. My player was undefeated and had won a close match previously in league over the challenger. In their second match up the challenger played great, winning the first set, but my player showed a very gritty competitiveness to win in three full grueling sets. The third set went all the way to a tiebreaker with our player winning 7-1. This match up began look very close. However, our #1 player continued to work on his speed around the court, and then he faced that same challenger again in the league finals. There was a moment where the challenger hit a great shot that nearly everyone was sure would be a winner, so they began to clap, but when my player arrived at the ball to hit it, they had to stop clapping. When the #1 seed then responded with a better shot, surprise became awe at how well he had moved. The #1 player won in a fairly routine straight sets victory along the lines of 6-3,6-2. I will always remember when the fans had to stop clapping, because a winner was not a winner.

CHAPTER THREE
Coaching Management Philosophy

Coaching really is an individual philosophy. ~ Mark Messier

Coaching a team is much like a family lifestyle. As a parent, you are there to lead, set examples, and keep your children on the right path. If you come into the job with a goal to be the player's friend, then you will almost immediately find trouble, especially when the players don't reciprocate. Start with a firm hand, or you may never gain managerial control of your team. Firm does not mean you have to have an iron fist. Going too far and losing your ability to listen and act wisely with your players can also make thing more difficult later. As a coach, you must find the style that works best for you and your team. I will explain what works for me, and I have seen coaches who appear to make other styles work for them. When I compare the longer term results of different styles I do believe what you find here will help you have more lasting success. John Wooden said, "I treat everyone the same, differently". I strongly suggest as you develop your system, that it have enough flexibility to meet players at their starting point and that you can work with the vast majority of them.

Since your coaching philosophy is so fundamental to the way the program is run, it's ideal if you can avoid any mistakes in forming your philosophy. Perhaps the two biggest mistakes I made in my coaching career were trying to be the friend of my players and running a democratic program. My first year as a coach, I was very friendly as a 26-year-old, and the result was that by the end of the season the team had very little cohesive planning and very little discipline in executing practices. The team had become subject to the whims of the players and what they felt like doing on a certain day. The easy going tone that I had set in my first year, made it more difficult the following year to take a more disciplined approach. If this is the situation you find yourself in as a coach, be sure to communicate early and often that a new approach will be taken in the next season. It was best for me to leave my first coaching position, then a few years later re-enter high school coaching at a different school.

When I was ready to re-enter the coaching world, I was determined not only to be more disciplined, but also to make it more fun. Over the course of a few seasons the totalitarian dictator approach really seemed to work well, then as the season wore on I would slowly shift into a benevolent monarch approach. Even after the best successes in 26 years at the school, an administrator urged me to try a more democratic approach. In that democracy captains would vote on activities   and players would give input. This lead to way too much time wasted in discussion, argument, and then when the minority did not get what they wanted, there were some attitude problems. The whole experience lead to creating a team that lacked unity. The results on court produced our worst finish in my six years at that school. The book, *Lord of the Flies* comes to mind, as I reflect on that year that started so poorly. By midseason I had to say "Democracy is over! You play on *my team*, and you are lucky to do so. Starting today, I run everything, although captains will have some input on which direction we take." Things slowly got better as we went along, but it was a difficult year for everyone because of my fateful decision to attempt democracy.

It is advisable to start with the most disciplined regimen, and then slowly loosen up because then you have established a baseline behavior you can go back to if needed.

The encouraging thing is that over time I have learned to start tough, and then very slowly become more and more permissive as the players gain my trust. More fun activities are introduced after the team shows a certain level of discipline, although even in the early going, I advise ending each practice with a brief, large group game. The first year is always the most difficult, especially if your approach is so much more disciplined than the coach who came before. I have experienced resistance from players and parents at every new coaching job, but after a period of time much greater acceptance as players become more successful. Remember that you are setting a foundation, and lay the groundwork for how the program will run for years to come. This is your program, and this is the best way to serve the players in the program for their ongoing success.

As the season continues the practices may become more and more fun, but then at the beginning of a new season, it's back to the same very disciplined approach. It's fascinating how teenagers forget how difficult the beginning of the season was in the previous year. I find my players telling others about how fun it is, and then I say, "Don't lie to them. Don't you remember the beginning? If they come the first two weeks, they'll think you lied to them." The new players who come the next season are fooled into thinking that the season is going to be a blast from beginning to end. Each new year the players come in happy because of the previous year's success, hopeful for more, and how fun it was at the end. They expect it to start that way the next year. I give them their rude awakening. We start with a slightly increased level of discipline in the second year, because now only the new players have to learn to get with the program. Those who are returning will be much more ready to take it up a notch.

Here are a few examples of a disciplined approach aimed at saving time and energy. The first is that on our courts we have a designated meeting court which is closest to the gate of entry. We always meet on the same court, and I always stand at the very corner of the court facing the sun. The players always make the best possible circle, so that everyone can see everyone, and not one player can hide behind another. Another example is that players, when we are practicing, would be spread out on six courts, on two banks of three courts. The kids on the far courts are the JV players and they have further to go. When I call them back to court 1 for a meeting, I expect everyone at the meeting court in 45 seconds. Why? Because if I wait for them it could take two to five minutes and in that time, they could be starting conversations with each other and getting distracted from what we are doing.

Finally an important discipline for coaches is to give regular water breaks. I make sure we have at least two five-minute water breaks. I also let everyone know that is the time for their conversation. I try to keep an eye on the players during this time and gauge how well people are getting along. Sometimes the conversation is good, and I see them truly bonding, so I extend the water break up to ten minutes. Team bonding is crucial for them to truly play for one another. As the season progresses, find a balance between togetherness, and hard work, fun, and discipline.

I have seen coaches who, because of their resume as a player, garner more respect from the outset, but you can't count on the kids to naturally know this--it must be shown on court. Those coaches may be more successful using a less-structured coaching style, but while I do see teams with coaches they truly like and are fun to be around at all times, I haven't seen the players having long-term lasting success in those programs. Ultimately, my best advice is to begin in the most disciplined possible way, ordering every action through the first two weeks of practice, then *slowly* ease back until the level of control is just right. Of course, there is a chance that undisciplined players may quit the team. For them I have two words: good bye. My guess is that you won't miss them much, and a clear message is sent to the rest of the team. One year, 25 girls came out for the team, and we got to work. Two weeks later there were only 11 girls left, all of whom improved dramatically, formed a very close-knit group, and became the nucleus for a team that would climb the standings. Imagine if the 14 girls who did not want to work had stayed? The 11 would not have gained the same benefit. I know this may run counter to the 'no-cut' increase the numbers approach, but what will happen in future years is that the team will grow and in a more healthy way with players who truly want to be there to become part of something that is very successful.

CHAPTER FOUR
Communication

The primary person with whom you will need to communicate is your athletic director. After you have taken all of the national certification training classes (usually online), the athletic director will train you on district and school policies. Normally you will be called to a meeting of all the coaches of your season of sport. Do all you can to build a strong bond with your AD and a trusting relationship, and your coaching career will be helped mightily. I have had some difficulty in this area, mainly due to my own failings, but sometimes it came from the athletic director. Just the same do your very best.

Communication with other coaches can be difficult as many lead busy lives doing many other things. If they are a teacher at the school, you might not be able to reach them during business hours. So communicate early and give plenty of time for a return call. In my area, the main concern is communication about the location of the match if its not at the school, and the total number of players attending the match. Failure to communicate can leave your players or their players without a match. That can be one of the most demoralizing part of high school play when the players don't get to play.

Communication with some teams and parents can be quite easy. In my current season, I have had 4 face to face contacts with parents, although at the beginning of the season I had called the parents of everyone on the team to let them know what to expect. I received very few calls back when I left a message. I have coached at other schools where a good percentage of parents are ever present, engaged and asking questions. Sometimes I don't enjoy answering their questions. A few things that you can do proactively that will save you a lot of time with communication is producing a calendar of events for the team, providing also all your contact information.

When it comes to the team I like to have a short meeting each day to discuss the schedule, and what we are trying to accomplish for the day. A quick 5 minute meeting each day goes a long way to keeping players on track.

If you have a fantasy that you can get away without communication early and often, then welcome to a miserable season: enjoy!

CHAPTER FIVE
Goal Setting

Stop setting goals. Goals are pure fantasy unless you have a specific plan to achieve them. ~ Stephen Covey

If you have some secret goals you don't share with the team, that can be very empowering for you. However, many times the personal goal of the coach can become a source of great pressure for the players. I usually have an outcome goal that keeps me challenged. I want the team to finish in the highest possible spot in the standings, or I may pick a team that may seem impossible to beat, and so that we can beat them. I never share my personal goals with my players, because I don't want them to feel added pressure to do that which does not look realistic. I want them to be surprised when they do it. For players, I want them to have their own personal goals, trying to climb the ladder. I want them all to understand that its great to have a few personal goals, but it is much more important for those to fall under the umbrella of team goals. I may tell a player that I want them to strive to be the #1 player not only for them, but for the team, because the challenge level to the #1 player makes the team better. If you improve and it forces the #1 player to improve, or fall to #2, either way the team is better for it.

One powerful goal that I start with every year is: We will be the most-improved team in the league. If you read and apply everything in this book, my goal is that your team *will* be the most-improved team in your league. Try this: at the beginning of the season plainly state, "We will be the most improved team in the league this year, and when we do that our chances of success go way up. Who's in?" You may be surprised at how the players buy into improvement. Your team is crucial to the goals you set. One particular team I coached was eager to put in the work, and I was confident with the goal that we set to become the most-improved team in our section of 143 teams. Certainly we could make a case for most-improved in the section, and also definitely among the most the very most improved in 450 teams in Northern California that year. While the judgement of improvement is hard to gauge, simply being in the conversation is a great outcome.

Improvement the key to success! Getting players more engaged in the process is more empowering to them. How do we manage that? I like to use a little nonsense, but for some reason it goes perfectly into the mind of a teenager and seems manageable.

- We will improve 100% this season

- We will improve 10% a week for 10 weeks

- Each week, we will become 2.5% more fit, have 2.5% better tactics and execution, our mental game will improve by 2.5%, we will become 2.5% better at executing our strokes.

- This sounds so doable, no?

- In reality, it's not so much that we improved our games 100%, but that we improved closer to the full potential of what is possible during 10 weeks, while other teams were not focused on improvement, but simply working on strokes and getting better only by playing 5 days a week. They improved only a fraction of what we did. One great thing about high school tennis is that every team will improve over 10 weeks simply aided by the fact that the players are playing 5 days per week.

- Here is a tale that proves a major improvement in one of my teams. I had heard that the coach of a league rival had guaranteed victory over my team, because we had lost our #1 player and six seniors from our doubles teams, completely wiping out our doubles lineup. Their team had added two very talented freshmen to the top of their lineup. We travelled to their school for the first match, and smelling blood in the water, they invited close to 100 fans to come watch their team beat our team, in our first meeting. My players felt very apprehensive, even though I was very confident we had enough talent to reload, instead of rebuild. But their nerves got the best of them when the other team came out on fire and nearly every player on their team was playing great. They seized a lead that could have led to a 4-3 victory for them. Our players responded to the challenge, steadied themselves with some gentle coaxing on my part, coming back and won some tough three-setters to win the match 5-2. Before the match was over many of the fans had already left. From the end of that match, motivated by the guarantee from the other coach, I wanted our team to put that second place team in our rear view mirror, and we then improved! That same league rival school never won more than one match against us in a dual match, and they never came close to holding a lead. We beat them 7-0 twice, and 6-1 once, moving forward. Yes, I was motivated by the promise of victory in the previous match.

Our team improved dramatically by succeeded in most all the goals listed below:

- We will perform the spider run agility drill with x number of players below 16 seconds, and x number of players below 15.4

- Players will memorize our mantra and pre-match goals

- The team will learn one major new strategy in singles and doubles, and work on it all season, so that in the second half of the season and playoffs it will be great.

- Learn a rolling topspin angle shot short and wide to pull the opponent off the court.

- Hit a high looping topspin to the backhand side, and in doubles poaching of the return of serve as the returning team.

Individual Performance goals:

- Player Z will serve 65% of first serves in play.

- Player Y will make 80% of his returns of serve.

- Player X will reduce his errors on the backhand by 50%.

- Player W will win 10% more points than before.

- Player V will learn a certain shot, so that he can perform a new shot combination.

- With each player, find their strength and set a goal to use that more often, find one weakness (and only one), and set a goal for it to be reduced as a liability. Players with a bad backhand can come to the net more or lob as a way to shore this up.

- "Whether I win or whether I lose, I stay motivated. If I win, I want to work hard to beat that player more easily next time. If I lose then its easy, I need to improve to beat that player" Bjorn Borg (paraphrase Bill Patton)

CHAPTER SIX
Growth Mindset

Without continual growth and progress, such words as improvement, achievement, and success have no meaning. ~ Benjamin Franklin

In recent years I have become more and more focused on personal growth, and for my students. In today's terminology, I have had a growth mindset ever since I abandoned my fixed mind set. The growth mindset is all about having a vision for what can be and moving towards it. Fixed mindsets see only talent and whats happening right now. I realize now that the more I have engaged in the life lesson aspect of coaching, the more buy in I get from my players, because they begin to participate in something long term. Placing too much pressure on the results of right now only serves to create an environment of fear. Players will fear losing, and will then play not to lose, instead of playing bravely learning how to win, playing to win, and participating in the process of growth.

There is a lot of social data that shows the value of sports participation on future success in life. One detail that might not get enough attention is how engaged were those people on their teams? Im my mind's eye I am imagining that those who are the ones who become very successful are the same ones who fully buy in on the process, are the leadership of the team, and cooperate fully with coaches to improve. These players don't need to be the most talented in order to succeed, simply the most dedicated.

I was trying to decide if I wanted to take a job coaching at a high school known for tremendous academic pressure on its students. In addition, from the outside the team looked like an underachieving team on the tennis court. They had a very strong lineup, and would win their league every year, then lose in the 1st round of the playoffs. The year before I arrived, the #1 player missed their playoff match, in order to take an AP test, which could have been rescheduled. So, I interviewed the returning players. "What do you want out of this team?" Answers "Win the league". So to each of the three players that I interviewed, I let them know that I am here to win a section championship. None of them really seemed as though they had thought about that before. When I was offered the job to coach this team, I was mainly interested because they had been a very talented team that had underachieved. I felt a certain responsibility to help guide them to performances that aligned more with what they could do if they showed some growth. In the first year we won league and entered the playoffs as a 9th seed out of 16, which meant facing the 8th seed on the road. So this would mean we are not favored to get out of the first round, however 8/9 is better than 7/10, or 6/11. Due to the fact that we had made a surge in improvement in the final weeks of the season we had a fairly routine 5-2 victory over the 8th seed. This drew some nice compliments from the other coach, but for me it was just our team playing pretty well. We had won the right to travel to the #1 seed.

When we arrived at the home of the #1 seed, a posh tennis club in Tiburon, CA which hosts posh professional tennis events, I felt defiant. Our team was going to play well even if we lost, we would bite, scratch, claw and gnaw our way through the match fighting for ever point. Out of the seven lines of play, they had three players against whom we had no realistic chance of winning a set, and winning a few games would be an accomplishment. During the warm up phase I over heard a very relaxed group of players and their parents discussing travel plans for the next round. There were other indicators that this team was taking us lightly.

Our strength was always our depth, as we had good players all through the lineup, but compared to other teams in our section we did not have superstars at the top of our group. Other teams had Division 1 scholarship talent, we did not. As we prepared, my assistant and I wrestled with the idea of making a lineup change to bolster our doubles lineup, but that would weaken us at #4 singles, and throw someone into a very tough situation at #4. When I announced to the team that we would be playing our normal line up, one player said "That's great coach, are you throwing in the towel?" I can't remember exactly what I said, but I do remember giving that player a playful punch on the shoulder, and expressing 'Of course not'. I explained that the other team and their parents were taking us lightly and didn't even go through a very good warm up, so I wanted them to really jump on them early and make the mother's cry.

Mother's did nearly cry, as our #4 player and all three doubles teams played incredible matches, maybe the match of their lives. #4 faced 4 match points, but eventually won 12-10 in the third set tiebreaker, (it was a full third set and the match took over 3 hours). We beat the #1 seed 4-3. Clearly this shows a level of growth from one season to the next. Later in the book is the story of our miracle win over MV which was the prohibitive favorite for the championship, but because that team underachieved in the final, we were able to win a section championship. But it was all based on growth.

CHAPTER SEVEN
Issues to Consider with Teenagers and Goal Setting

The principle goal of education in the schools should be creating men and women who are capable of doing new things, not simply repeating what other generations have done. ~Jean Piaget

Outcome and Process Oriented Goals
Process oriented goals should account for the bulk of all goal setting, but an outcome of beating a certain player, team, or to make a certain round of a tournament are all fine goals. Making goals SMART is very important, additionally the values behind the goals can be the most empowering and remove some of the fear from the goal setting.

Specific, **M**easureable, **A**chievable, **R**ealistic, and **T**imely.

Example: Improving My First Serve %.

I will get my first serve % to 65% by the first day of the league season.

I will have a match where I don't miss a serve.

Values: When a player writes down why they want to achieve the goal it could reflect such things as: to gain confidence, to challenge my teammates, to make the team better, to increase my chance of success, to reduce my fear of_____,

Activities:

1. Take a lesson and practice form that supports high %

2. Practice serving at 70%

3. Practice a variety of serves will still serving at 70%

4. Play simulated practice games while maintaining 70%

5. Play a practice set at 65% or greater.

6. Play a live competitive set measure progress.

7. Repeat steps 1-6 as necessary.

Outcome Goal:

Beat the Player that I lost 7-5,6-4 at our next match.

Identify where my points were lost, where my points where won, how he or she won their points or lost their points.

Identify the most realistic shots where errors can be reduced or new tactics can create more offense.

Note: it may be unrealistic in a the span of a few weeks to beat someone who beat you by score greater than 6-2,6-2. Gauge how much better you can play, or how close to the absolute peak the other player was in the previous match.

Sometimes a great goal is to win more games, but given no-ad scoring some score outcomes don't represent how close a match might have been.

Process Goals: Strengths and Weaknesses

Depending on the player, I work on the strength first because it acknowledges the player and affirms they have good things to offer in their game. Shortly thereafter we look at the weakness. Some coaches treat every shot like a weakness, or try to work on every aspect of a player's game. "Break 'em down to build 'em up" It's not wise to have your players in broken-down mode for 10weeks. Additionally, if you start work on the weakness and you are not successful getting it fixed in the first three or four weeks of the season, it's best to leave it alone and find a way to tactically work around it. You do not build a champion by having a player enter every match worried that his weakness may make him lose. How you approach this depends on the relationship you have with the player, their maturity level, and what the true priorities are for game improvement.

Player Motivation Intrinsic v. Extrinsic

One of the most important transformations that can happen with an athlete that will help them in later life is learning to be intrinsically motivated. Pat something said "A very large group of athletes at my Division I university are still playing to please their parents. They don't know the freedom of playing for their own joy".

CHAPTER EIGHT
Rules and Consequences

I believe in rules of behavior, and I'm quite interested in stories about the consequences of breaking those rules. ~John Irving

How do your rules and consequences fit with your coaching philosophy? When setting the rules and consequences, it's best to remember the life lessons that come along with them and the values that your coaching philosophy sets forth. If they don't match up, then there is an incongruence that will lead to confusion for your players. When everything lines up, players can make better decisions. I know coaches who are very kind, but have very harsh rules and consequences. Conversely, there are coaches who are very harsh and forbidding, but run a very loose and inconsistently administered team. Both can be disasters for the educational experience of the player, and can turn them off from the sport. Consider that how you set the parameters of the team has an effect on the mission, objectives, and goals of the team. They also set a tone for what you will accept and not accept. It's best to be authentic, and avoid setting a rule that you do not plan to enforce. Most excellent is to only have rules you will enforce 100% of the time with very few exceptions. On the other hand, no set of rules is ever perfect, and you should always reserve the right to decide case by case. Player's can be caught in some circumstances that were outside of their control. Few things are more demoralizing to a teenager than to be punished for something over which they had no control so, use your best judgement. In addition players who show sincere sorrow for their failings, it would best to show at least some mercy to them.

No matter how restrictive or permissive you are, it is important to have the proper amount of rules that fit the needs of the team. Without rules, there is no game. In social psychology there is ample research to support the idea that a few great rules consistently enforced gives teenagers a greater sense of security and has a positive impact on morale because they know where the lines are drawn. Any rule that is not enforced should not be a rule. Keep the rules simple so you can avoid acting as a cop, lawyer, or judge. Even more important is to have consequences that make sense and address the behavior, and then do something to create character where it was found lacking.

Here are some rules that are paramount. I recommend three to five rules.

1. **Be on time to practice** every day, and practice starts precisely at the time allotted. Therefore, you the coach must also be ready to start practice on time. A lot of time is wasted over a season when practice does not start on time or players don't start on time. One player coming in a minute last is a match that starts the fire. Four players coming three minutes late is a fire starting to spread. Seven players coming five minutes late is a forest fire. Put out the match before it becomes a forest fire. Here I like to add more warm-up laps to the agenda of the late player. If they do it again, I will have a long talk with them and also give them a bad court assignment for the early going or for a full day. One player's attendance was so poor that I let her know if she missed work that same amount, she would be fired. Later, she had the nerve to ask me for a job teaching tennis in my summer program.

2. **Give 100% effort at all times.** "95% effort is usually good for second place in a match." This one is obvious, but not easy to

enforce, and you need to truly understand your team and know your players to detect a drop in effort. One great piece of advice I received on this is that effort is not what *I* see as much as it is the perception of the player. It is mostly the player's perception that needs to change, but sometimes it is the coach's. When meeting a new player and seeing what I think is a low-effort level, I ask the player, "Is that 100% effort?" The answer may surprise you. I then say, "To me it looked like less than 100%. Please do the action one more time, and I want to see you giving your all." They always do. If they do exactly the same thing, then that is their 100%. Everyone is wired differently. At least 90% of the time, I see an uptick in the intensity, and that's when I can say, "See, *that* is your 100%--or at least closer to it". Jim Loehr, sport psychologist, says that giving 100% effort is vital in developing a great mental game. It is extremely difficult to give 100% effort during an entire match without having a few points at 95%. Help players understand, self monitor, and develop their own discipline. Team captains and top players need to know that they help set a strong example in this area.

3. **Respect for everyone.** Disrespectful talk from player to player, player to coach, or coach to player is not acceptable. I myself have sometimes used some coarse joking, and then wished I had not said certain things and apologized. Over the years, I have worked very hard to consider my past mistakes prior to saying something that could be construed the wrong way. Mutual respect is fundamental to creating an atmosphere of unity. Without respect for one another, attempts at unity are meaningless because the "why" has been removed from the equation. Everyone must respect in words, deeds, and in their physical body, by no offending each other or having unwanted contact.

4. **Communication.** Players communicate with the coach themselves and must not send intermediaries do their communicating, including parents. Part of what is taught is mature

behavior. An exception is when the player is extremely ill and then the parent can call. In this day and age with a multitude of ways to communicate, I still expect a player to call me on the phone for this kind of communication.

5. **Everyone must stay and watch while the varsity match is still in progress.** Some teams allow players to leave as soon as they finish their match. When they stay and cheer on their teammates, they learn that if they get into a tough match, they will have someone cheering for them. There are few things more shameful than a home tennis match where one player from the home team is playing, while most or all of his teammates have gone home. And if playing against a road player who has all his fans there-- ouch. Younger players must learn to pay their dues in this way so as to earn the right of the same type of support. Additionally, they learn much more about the sport by seeing these matches played.

6. **Decisions must be thoughtful, avoid acting on whims.**.I will let your mind reel on the concept of helping teenagers become better decision makers on court and in regard to their contribution to the team. (Take a deep breath coaches, who have experience with teenagers!)

The above categories for rules act as a guideline for you to create your own specificrules. I recently heard of a tennis academy that created some very restrictive rules for their program and tournaments that they hold. My first reaction to reading the very detailed and lengthy list of banned behaviors had me feeling like it was going to be no fun. Also, my own rebellious nature began to kick in and I was thinking about how if applied to me, I would rather be in another program that allowed some of those behaviors. Remember that you may be working with players from all walks of life, and overly restrictive rules may hurt your team and program more than help. So, be very judicious in how you approach the development of your rules and consequences.

Dress Code: I had a conversation today with Mike Baugh a high school coach in Florida about the importance at some schools of establishing a dress code. A word of warning, this can be a very touchy issue, especially as it touches on a cultural clash between teenagers, adults and schools. Some students see the way they dress as a first amendment right, but we all now that the first amendment has to do with free speech and not free dress. One other consideration is that the coach must be very skillful in addressing any standard. It's very easy for a teenage girl to ask "Why are you looking there?". It's also not easy for a teenage boy to understand why he might not be able to play without a shirt. So, work closely with your AD, and perhaps at the beginning of a new season create a new standard stating that players will dress modestly without plunging necklines, and wear shorts, a short or skirt over any compression gear. It can't be emphasized enough that the coach must be extremely careful in the way they approach this issue.

CHAPTER NINE
Carefully Targetted Consequences

In this life, we have to make many choices. Some are very important choices. Some are not. Many of our choices are between good and evil. The choices we make, however, determine to a large extent our happiness or our unhappiness, because we have to live with the consequences of our choices.
~James E. Faust

Be masterful in this area of administering consequences, and you gain the trust and respect of your team. Everything you do should support and promote a commitment to the team. Fail in this area, and morale will suffer--immediately. If you are heavy-handed in the relationships you have with players and/or the team and you will rob the joy from the process. One consequence I hate is, "If you miss practice, you must miss the next match." If it happens to be your top player, and tomorrow you play your rival in what you expect to be a tough match, will you make your team lose to prove a point? Don't do it! Why would you want to ruin your season, when you could easily find a more severe consequence that does not affect the team?

Better Consequences:

1. "If you miss practice unexcused, you will miss a match of my choice." This way I can strategically use that to help a younger

player, and take away what really hurts--an easy win for the player! Teenagers can be great at accepting the challenge of a tough match, but an easy win can be the most enjoyable thing for them. Let someone more deserving have it.

2. Punish only the player responsible for their action. Punishing a whole group of people for the infraction of one is counterproductive. The only exception would be if there was a known conspiracy between players to assist a player who had done something seriously negative to the team experience.

3. When explaining possible consequences, I like to say "If you surprise *me* with bad news, I may surprise *you* with bad news." The form this usually takes is that a player has skipped practice or a match with a lame excuse or not enough notice for something to be done. I most commonly have them come on the bus to a road match. When I announce the lineup, their name is not in it. This works very well, but only if you follow up with the player. "How did it feel to be here to play, but find out you were not in the lineup? How do you think I feel when I plan to have you in the lineup, and you are not there? It's the same. I am doing this so you can develop empathy. The best possible thing you can do is take it well, and cheer on your teammates here. You owe them your best." Open this up to a discussion. Usually the player understands, and I see a much stronger commitment from them. I normally only do this when a player has had multiple infractions.

Make your own consequences that are really targeted at teaching life skills. Many times our consequences are not strong enough, and sometimes they take a scorched earth approach. Taking the time to decide each case separately and 'coaching everyone the same, differently' can really help the team when you expertly address each player in the best possible way for what they need.

In my current season of play, many new players joined the team, but they had no idea about the commitment level we were looking for. Rather than punish them, and/or dismiss them, I began to simply remind them that we have practice 5 days a week, and we are making a commitment. Also, as they walk in late, I ask them what time practice starts, and then ask what is the current time. After two full weeks of this and one day where more than half the team came late, I gave them a speech about `commitment. I asked the captains to talk with the team to come up with a consequence. So the team came up with making the late players do a grueling conditioning exercise with everyone watching. I live by the rule 'never punish with exercise', because it makes young people think of exercise as punishment. So, I got to be the nice guy, and came up with this. Late players will miss the first 5 minutes of group games, and if everyone is at practice on time, game time will be extended by 5 minutes.

CHAPTER TEN
The 7 Deadly Sins

1. Too Much Work on Technique and at the Wrong Time - Coaches sometimes place too much emphasis on technique to the point where their players never feel completely confident in their strokes, as though they always need to do better. It can have them feeling that they are not good enough to win. Intuitively, it seems that if doing some work on technique is good, then working more will be better. On the day you play, your game is your game, and you as a player need to play with the confidence that you know what you bring to the table. Having unsettled strokes can lead to uncertainty, and fear of making a mistake. As you proceed into a pivotal part of your schedule, STOP working your strokes and instead play points. Anywhere from 3 days to 2 weeks prior to the meat of our schedule where all the crucial matches lie, I avoid giving any major technical advice, but I may give one small tip here or there. Sometimes a player simply needs to be reminded of what makes their stroke better based on something that has already been learned. Allow players to use what they have in a practice match situation a few times to see if the changes have taken hold. If they have not taken hold in a player's game, why would you pressure them to use those changes against top competition? Making any major change to a stroke prior to intense competition can leave a player with a very unsettled feeling, and lacking confidence to perform under pressure. The only exception would be a beginner who is lacking an important stroke the day before competition begins. Depending on the athleticism and personality of the player, you may want to hold out a beginner from competition until they learn enough technique to serve, return and hold a rally.

2. Tennis is largely an **anaerobic sport**, so the largest chunk of a player's training should be anaerobic. The playing of tennis matches provides much of the aerobic fitness for a tennis player. The Preparation Phase in the periodized schedule is usually 4-6 weeks, but there is not time for that in a high school season, so athletes should complete that phase prior to the season. **Many coaches spend too much time on aerobic training.** A case can be made that players may lose quickness on the court when trained too much for aerobic capacity. Additionally, I know some teams that put a lot of effort into aerobic fitness, but then my teams are stronger and faster in the third set when the other teams anaerobic stores are used up. When the players play plenty of tennis, then they gain the necessary threshold of aerobic fitness to play. If your practices are two hours and active nearly the whole time, with some intense bouts, playing a match should not be that much harder. I have been very successful with a very minimum of aerobic training. The minimum amount of aerobic activity to produce aerobic training is 12 minutes of exercise. In the first few weeks of the season, I will have the players run for 12 minutes. When everyone can get through 12 minutes without walking, then we have the necessary base. The remainder of our training is in the anaerobic area, which is harder to train, and requires a coach to supervise to make sure the intensity is high enough.

3. Coaches schedule too few matches for their team. Getting your team dialed in before the start of your league season can only really be accomplished through match play. No matter how well your practice, the first team match of a season can be a very nervous experience for players. All the practice matches against familiar foes can give a false sense of security, because the anxiety of "Now it Counts" is not present. Also, after you see the players playing a few matches, you can see the reality of what they are doing, so you can adjust your plan.

4. Coaches may fail to stick to their periodized schedule plan.
When you create a periodized schedule stick to it. Recently, I had a huge influx of beginners onto a team, and it was tempting to change the plan away from the 'competition' phase, but instead I stayed with that phase of training with the rest of the team, while teaching beginners on the fly, giving them just enough information to get the ball in their racquets. Diverting the plan of the team for the needs of a few is not a good idea. Also, you most likely will find that some pre-season results are affected negatively when you are in Pre-Competition Phase. Players will pick up on that and it naturally leads to second guessing. "Coach, we need to win this match to get a better seeding in playoffs", "Player, we need to train so that we will perform so well in the playoffs that our seeding won't matter. Besides, I would rather be seeded too low, than be seeded too high. Assume the underdog role". In playoff action, my team's have defeated two teams seeded higher!

5. Speaking of Matches as "Must Win". Players already feel a tremendous amount of pressure to win. They may also feel pressure to win for you, the coach. Piling on more pressure can be the what takes a player or team to the breaking point. While Billie Jean King said "Pressure is a privilege", a well noted study of elite athletes in every major professional sport reported that 85% agreed that "when I feel pressure, I perform worse." Other outcome goals like winning championships, or league titles or beating certain players can create pressure. When coaches continually discuss outcome goals, it can bring quite a load of pressure to bear on teenagers. My outcomes have been increasingly better in my coaching career, as I learn better who to engage players in the process of improvement. Getting better increases your chance of winning, right? So instead, guide your players along that path, and let them surprise you with great performances.

6. Coaches stick too closely to their plan without making a necessary adjustment. If you have only 10 weeks during the season, realize it is a very short window to accomplish what you can. I strongly recommend that you have a detailed plan for the first few weeks of practice before you begin day one. After a few days, reflect and modify your plan to fit the team. After a short while, ask the team captains how they think things are going, and what the players are saying. Make sure your team captains understand more about the specific plan. Maybe you realized that you are trying to cram too much into those 10 weeks, so ease the pressure by trimming some non-essentials out of the program. In reality, there is not a lot that can be done in 10 weeks, but if you focus on the essentials for success, then it can be managed. Instead of trying to accomplish 20 objectives in 10 weeks, pare it down to 5: team unity, mental game, strategy and tactics, stroke work, conditioning and fitness.

7. Playing Favorites with Players, or Focusing too much Energy on too few Players. It's a bad idea to play favorites. Think back to when you were a kid, for me it was demoralizing to put in a lot of work, but not gain the attention of the coach, because they had already selected their favorites.   If you are paying forward the torture you received as a teenager, think about it and change your ways. "We had to do it this way!" is not a great reason to do something in less than the best way. There are many high school coaches who are not at all mindful of the fact that they spend way too much time with the better players, or with the more engaging personalities on the team, that's easy to do. They have no idea the negative impact that has on the team as a whole, as players seem to vie for attention, or give up trying to engage the coach. It's as though the coach is acting out a sub-conscious thought that certain players bring them glory, and others do not, so they will focus their time and energy on those who do. What's missing here is that some otherwise seemingly untalented players go undeveloped, and some personalities that would emerge, if engaged, fail to emerge, because of that neglect. Of course, you may need to spend a bit more time with certain players for whatever reason, but be mindful of engaging everyone on the team.

CHAPTER ELEVEN
How to Avoid Mistakes

Creating and achieving one strong outcome from each of the five objectives in the previous chapter will create a very strong season. Every season these five areas must be addressed. I recommend to stress three or four of them each day, so one or two can have a rest. Work your plan so that the largest and most important topics are covered first, and then move to more subtle topics. Of course, in different phases of training, some of these will be discontinued or reduced.

Take out a calendar, put in every match date, and you will see how many days you have for practice. Of course, for some teams tryouts take up a large portion of time, but even for those days, you need a plan for those players who are a lock to make the team. I like to schedule the maximum number of dual matches with other teams, and I can if I have a team that is excellent or pretty good with few or no beginners. Generally, I will have the maximum amount of competitive matches on the schedule allowed by rule and will use any allowance in the rules for the absolute greatest amount of play. One year we had 26 matches! It was truly an amazing experience and I saw tremendous growth in my team because of the regular outlet found in the challenge of competition. That season strongly affirmed how much players want to play, and they want the match experience. Give it to them! They will also be more receptive to learning if you have identified something in a match on which they need to work.

If the team has quite a few beginners or is a bottom-rung team, even so schedule at least four pre-season matches so the first league match has a mid-season feeling to it. If pre-season matches are not realistic, find ways to get your players to compete against strangers in the two weeks leading up to your season. Many states have invitational tournaments that are run in either a team or individual format. One of my teams filled with very new players played the largest high school tennis tournament in the nation. Our players had a great team even though we competed in Division 9, the lowest of all the divisions. I promise you that more matches will be more fun, and practices will be less boring if preceded or followed by matches on the other days. Five straight days of practice can become quite dull.

CHAPTER TWELVE
Daily Planning - Balance

Another problem that many coaches fall into is not finding the right balance between working on player's games, and fun. Some days a practice could be under programmed, other days too many objectives that crowd out the fun. Imagine filling a glass with water, and you want to leave a little room so you won't spill. Some coaches plan to put more water into the glass than can possibly fit, and then it becomes a mess. They then sacrifice the fun part of practice for more work, and that will lead to poor morale.

I usually plan a practice so if everything went perfectly we would have a jam-packed practice full of great things to do and a fun ending. I will not sacrifice the fun ending, even if we did not achieve our full objectives. The only exception to that is when there is some kind of behavioral issue or injury. In line with best consequences, I rarely recommend canceling the fun part of practice because of the actions of one or two players. If a certain objective was not met, then a decision needs to be made whether to adjust the plan on future days. so that we will finish up that objective on the next practice. It's your plan, so change it if you want to. Don't tell the players the full details of the plan, but be honest if something is not going to according to plan. They will respect your honesty.

CHAPTER THIRTEEN
Daily Planning - Facets of Training

I love the De La Salle High School Football Program. The movie "When the Game Stood Tall" is a movie out that will show perhaps the most difficult season during that high school football team's great era of success. Perhaps the most important aspects of what they teach in that program are mastery and discipline, the template of what they do can be recreated in nearly any sport.

De La Salle runs 12 plays on offense. The vast majority of high school football teams attempt to run 2 to 8 times as many plays. When De La Salle practices, they practice one play over and over again--much longer than 99% of other schools. They will run that play, not only until it's very good and works almost every time, but until every foot of every player goes exactly in the right place. In contrast, many other teams will continue a practice well beyond the allotted time as punishment for not having learned the play. De La Salle simply picks it up the next day and continues to practice.

What does "picking it up tomorrow" have anything to do with tennis? We need to develop our daily practice routines to make sure the players learn mastery, and of course it takes discipline to gain mastery.

There are four things that are commonly a part of almost every practice:

1. Fitness

2. Strategy and Tactics

3. Situational Play or Match Play

4. Stroke Work

As discussed previously, every day's practice must fit with the phase of training. Rarely will all four of the above happen in the same practice. This is why you must plan well to make sure to include each of the above in the best phase at the ideal time.

CHAPTER FOURTEEN
Periodized Planning

Periodizing a schedule is not very difficult. There are macro and micro periodization plans. I recommend you stay with macro, as in Keep It Simple. However, an exception may be made for a player who played three or more matches over the weekend. There schedule could be micro periodized for a day or two. I recommend a micro periodization that does not place a tired player through a tough workout like the others. Why make your most motivated players exhausted? If anyone from among that player's teammates complains, then I ask them, "Raise your hand if you played three or more tournament matches over weekend," and that usually settles any complaints. If you can get the players to do some aerobic training prior to walking on the court, that's an important part. If you have a 10-week season, that can be limiting. If your team is very successful and expects to play up to 12 weeks, then that frees you up a bit on the front-end schedule.

However, if you extend the preparation phase too deep into the schedule, players will second-guess the wisdom. It goes like this: "Coach, why are we doing all this? Don't we have a match tomorrow against a team that if we beat them we'll get a better seeding in playoffs?"

My answer: "When else can we get this work done? It's now or never. Also, seedings are irrelevant. Imagine we are working hard now, and that team is resting. If we can beat them now, our seed is assured. If not, we'll beat them when it matters most--in the playoffs. Besides, I would rather be seeded too low and motivated by it than seeded artificially high and have unrealistic expectations while not being fit enough at the end. And yes, I want to win a section title no matter what we are seeded."

Having dealt with the push-back from players and parents when they don't understand, its important to be transparent and have the best possible and as air-tight a plan and you can create. It's also good to verbally share with the team the details of the plan. I would not show it in writing, but when they question it, you can let them know you have a plan, and you would be happy to explain it again to the whole team. It never comes to that. In greater detail, periodization goes like this:

CHAPTER FIFTEEN
Phases of Training

1.　　**Preparation Phase** (This should take 4 to 6 weeks and better teams should only take 3 weeks.　　　　　Expect players to do this on their own prior to the season.)

- aerobic training, longer continuous drills, some running (less than 3 miles)

- Full body workouts, stretching, core training

- Stroke work (one strength, one weakness)

- Team routines

- Mental game foundations

- Review basic strategies

- Identify player's game styles

- Players may be sore, tired, not fully confident in their game.

- **2.　　Pre-Competition Phase** (2 to 4 weeks)

- Point play situations increase (Special Sets, Pressure Sets)

- Core conditioning continues and plyometric explosive training commences.

- Aerobic warm up continues, aerobic training emphasis tapers or ends

- Challenge matches lineup takes shape

- By end of this phase, lineup may be set

- Deeper strategies - Build on foundation of basics, add one tactic

- Specific mental skills based on early point play

- Stroke work diminished or eliminated, practice increased

- May overlap with early season matches, results may be diminished

- **Competition Phase** (1 week, 10 days, 2 weeks)Fit this to your schedule! I have had competitive phases that only lasted 5 days.

- Practice and point play only, focus is on a cluster of targeted matches, or match with rival - practice sets (special rules?)

- Minimize any new information

- Limit conditioning or do none

- The objective is to have players rested and tuned in for play

- Maximum 3 comp phases in a season, with one being post-season

- For young or low-skilled teams, 2 comp phases are advisable mentally and emotionally (pick the second match against rival as one to target)

- 4. **Active Rest Phase** (1 to 2 days or more if a weekend approaches)

- After the last of the cluster matches, or rival match

- Fun day, loose practice, lots of games

- Nothing serious

- Time to reflect on the outcomes win or lose

- Never threaten to take this away because of bad outcome

- "There is nothing you can do in the comp phase that will cause me to take away active rest fun day."

- Team will trust you and play harder moving forward

- Empowers effort, because players know rest is coming

- Games, games, games

- Nobody skips

- Nobody devalues the experience

- Talk about the next phase

CHAPTER SIXTEEN
The Second Round of Phases

At the completion of the active rest day(s) phase of the season, you may return to the Preparation Phase for a few days, or go back to Pre-Competition phase. The second time around, the Pre-Competition Phase will be shorter. In the second half of your season, select the match or close cluster of matches in your competitive phase, and make sure the Competition Phase allows for at least two practices in that mode. Again, upon completion of that phase, you will want to have at least one and probably only one day of active rest phase. One thing I noticed preparing for the post-season sectional playoffs is how tired my teams have become. I'm in the habit of having a light optional practice the day after a playoff win. With extremely difficult matches every other day, culminating in two on the same day to win, rest became much more important than practice. By that time, everyone's game was as dialed in as much as it was going to be. There will be some days you wish you could finish up what you are teaching, but if you can send the players home happy with a fun time in the last 15 to 20 minutes of practice each day, that will have tremendously positive effect. Always remember that young people play sports because they are fun, and they want to improve and be with friends. While you may have an airtight plan, make sure the one thing that is most airtight is the fun aspect.

CHAPTER SEVENTEEN
Tiebreakers

"Failure to prepare is preparing to fail." General George S. Patton

So few pieces of the tennis game are as vital to the battle of winning a match as being successful in tiebreakers. When you play your closest competition, the likelihood that tiebreakers will be played and could be the deciding factor in a match is an inescapable fact. For this reason I include more tiebreaker play into my practices than set play. Players will easily get into the groove of playing a set. However, up to 90% of high school players either are uncomfortable playing, or don't really know how to play a tiebreaker. What will that do to their confidence in a match when they are headed into a crucial part of the competition and not know what they are doing. I find that my player's relative experience and comfort level in a tiebreaker allows them many times to take charge of the tiebreaker. This gives them a huge psychological advantage over the opponent who does not know them, and/or does not practice tiebreakers often.

I like to get four players together for a round robin of tiebreakers. Sometimes you will notice that certain players who might not be able to beat someone in a full set actually has an advantage in a tiebreaker either because they serve or return serve so well.

CHAPTER EIGHTEEN
Fitness and Mental Game

"Gentlemen, legs feed the wolf "~ Herb Brooks

When using a 10-week season, it is far more profitable to invest the maximum amount of energy that the players can give into fitness, without getting injured. Early in my coaching career I pushed my player too hard, but some of them got hurt, and it slowed their development. Oddly, they bought into it, when they started to really enjoy being an athlete, instead of just a tennis player. When I scaled back the work to a very efficient level, some players were disappointed that I did not destroy them, and felt I had gone soft.

A 10-week or longer athletic season done well is exhausting for players the first time they go through it, so consider how you want to finish. Keep in mind the goal is to be conditioned for the season. Conditioning wisely increases the likelihood that your players will out last, out run, and/or over power their competition.

I want my team to be most fit and have the most energy as we enter the post-season, but you have to make the investment at the beginning so you can make the withdrawal in the form of competitive performance at the end of your successful campaign when it matters most. In the early going, fitness may be 25% of practice, then as we get to midseason it may taper to about 10% with some well timed bouts of high intensity work, and then we get close to post-season it drops to 0%.

The Mental Game - Based on Solid Principles

If you don't feel qualified to teach the mental game, be sure to get great some great books. I strongly recommend anything by Jim Loehr. His older books, while dated, are still very relevant and are reflected as an influence in this title. Be sure to spend five minutes per day working, talking, thinking and asking about the mental game. I start by teaching my players about our process goals:

1. Give 100% effort

2. Enjoy the competition

3. Show yourself strong and wise

4. Learn from every match and practice

63% of points are won when you approach the net to the other player's backhand

CHAPTER NINETEEN
Developing Strategy and Tactics

It's a great idea to have a daily talk for no more than 5 minutes about a nuance of strategy and tactics, starting with the most basic, then more and more detailed as you go along in the season. Plan a five-minute lecture, followed by top players on your team modeling the tactic. Of course, be sure to select players who are very capable of showing how to do a certain tactic. A very high percentage of high school matches are won simply with a high first serve percentage and cross court groundstroke play. Have players practice it. One common frustration among high school coaches is how rarely the players come to the net. Shared recently by Craig O'Shannessy of Brain Game Tennis, "Of all the data from the recently completed U.S. Open, men's and women's matches combined, it was discovered that 63% of points are won when you approach the net to the other player's backhand." This completely annihilates the notion that pro players can't come to the net successfully, and our high school players certainly do not hit passing shots better than professional players. High school tennis is not pro tennis. While your very best players may face another player with incredible topspin passing shots, they can still come in to the net.

The solution? Make a commitment as a coach to go through the entire process of building a new tactic into your playe's games. Start on day one with net drills. I have players play at the net every day, until nearly 100% of my players are comfortable coming to net.

Impossible, you say? You don't know my team.

Here is a progression by which you can add a new tactic to your player's game. Also, when you read this far, simply join my email list and I will send you a video of a presentation I gave on "Getting Your Team to the Net". First, you must know their fears, they are afraid to lose because they tried something new. They are afraid to look like they don't know what they are doing. Players can be very frightened to make a mistake, losing a point instantly, or feel like they don't have enough time to see the ball. They are afraid of the unknown, and the responsibility to always do a certain thing. They may also be afraid of a new level of success and how they will respond. This progression helps them get past much of that, and then you will need to use your own creativity as a coach to solve any problems along the way:

1. Start with a no-pressure warm up. A simple approach shot/volley drill with no negativity directed at the players. Allow them to begin to get comfortable.

2. A drill with targets on the court, with the coach taking notes as to who needs to work on which aspects of the volley. Giving the players 5 minutes of volley instruction, and simply praising those who make an improvement goes a long way toward building player confidence.

3. Step 1, Step Two, then some more detailed drills, approaching to the backhand, volleying short crosscourt to the opposite side.

4. A warm-up, instruction, drill, point play without recording win or loss. Players can play points out without anyone winning a competition, you can rotate players to act as the passing shot artist. It can be wise to start with a middle of the road player on the team as the baseline player to allow players some confidence coming in, prior to allowing better and better players to be at the baseline.

5. Step 1-4 (or skip steps), then play "Rule the Court" where a challenger who wins three points becomes the new champion. I might do this on two or more courts with three challengers on each court. Each time a new champion is crowned, the old champion moves up one court. When a new champion comes to the top court, the challenger with the fewest points goes all the way to the end court. The great thing about this game is that players will gain confidence as they move up the courts, if you sprinkle the better players throughout the courts, then they must win their way onto higher courts. If you did this on three courts, I would put players #6 and #3 on court one, #5 and #2 on court two, and #4 and #1 on court three, or something along those lines.

6. This is a critical step, if you feel like the players still need confidence repeat whichever steps 1 through 5 that you feel may be helpful. In this step have players play tie-breakers where the server gets one serve and the returner must come to the net. The rule I use, is that the returner must be inside the service box before the point is won in order to gain the point. The interesting thing is that I rarely enforce that rule, and usually only when a player makes no effort to come forward. Be sure to spend a few minutes warming up serves. If they are fairly confident from what came before, just warm them up a bit and allow them to warm up serves prior to playing. Don't worry that the initial tiebreakers will not be very pretty, as this level of pressure is something they might not be used to playing under. Discuss how it feels to serve a second serve and follow up with a passing shot right away. Most likely the first few tiebreakers will be a little rocky. After three tiebreakers, anyone who still is not doing well may repeat steps 1–5.

7. Play tie-breakers with two serves, but returner must come to net on second serve. This then requires players to remember the game plan. They also will need to shift mentally from a defensive mind set of returning first serve, to an offensive mindset of attacking second serve.

8. Play practice sets, and notice how easily players begin to come into the net. There will be a time when a player easily recognizes that a ball was inside the service box, move easily forward and attack the net. One very obvious aspect of tennis is that the serve by necessity has to be a short ball. When your players begin to attack those short balls, be sure to notice. If you praise them for it, they are much more likely to do it again and again.

CHAPTER TWENTY
Technical Solutions to Tactical Problems

With no much focus on so called modern tennis, there has been an enormous fascination in technique at the pro level. Amateur players then seek to mimic their favorite tennis professionals. While the better high school players can have technique that closely resembles professional players, they often miss out on the tactics that win high school tennis matches. The strategies and tactics that won high school matches in the last century, still win very many matches in this century. A few tactics that have seen their rise in use more often are heavy looped topspin shots that push opponents back behind the baseline. The way that has changed is the speed and spin of the shot has increased with poly string and racquets more suited to spin. That tactic can still be called moon balling, although its effectiveness has improved significantly. Moon ball players were generally regarded as not being able to beat you, they would wait for you to beat yourself. Now they can beat you. Rafael Nadal the prime example of this style of play answered a question at a recent press conference about his strategy, he said something to the effect of, "I play a lot of heavy topspin to my opponent's backhand, pretty simple, no?". Of course when Nadal receives a weak reply from that shot, he is able to hit other more offensive shots.

Really truly, how many high school players have the physicality to deliver what Nadal delivers in speed and spin. Not very many, so a patient player can defeat that style if they understand the technical side of solving tactical problems.

It's still true that its easier to reduce errors in your game than it is to increase the amount of winners and forcing shots without adding even more errors to ones game. Even though this is fairly simply stated and easy to follow the complexity lies in coaching players who are naturally gifted with offensive weapons in their game, but who are afraid to make a few mistakes, so they play cautiously when really they should play bravely, accept a few mistakes because the risk reward ratio is good for them.

CHAPTER TWENTY-ONE
Favorite Games and Drills

Pressure Sets - This is more a game for top players, because it can be very frustrating to play. The rules are simple. If you get to game point as the server, or the receiver, you must win that point, or instead, you lose all your points. So, if you are ahead 40-30 in a game and lose the next point, then next point would be Love-30. The opponent does not gain a point if you lose your game point. This game really encourages players to focus on a game point!

Forehands Only - I like this game early in the season to re-establish a crosscourt game play mentality.   This can be a little complicated. Players start the rally with a feed, and play crosscourt only, along the diagonal from the right hand side of the court playing only forehands, to the other player's forehand court. If a ball goes on the wrong side of the court, or long then the opponent wins one point. However, if the ball goes into the net or wide in the alley or further, then the opponent gets 2 points. You might be amazed at how quickly players will give up consecutive 2 point plays to their opponent. You can modify this game to allow for one backhand per point.

Defend Your Backhand - Start your best player with the best backhand as the champion. They must only hit backhands, although you can change the rule to allow one forehand. Challengers must hit only into the half of the court that is the champion's backhand area. Champions, however, are allowed to hit anywhere in the Challenger's singles court, and Challenger's can hit backhands and forehands. The point starts with a coach feeding a ball to the Challenger's backhand, and they must hit a backhand to begin the point.

One Bounce Doubles - A great game for intermediate to advanced doubles players to encourage them to take the ball out of the air as much as possible. After the serve goes in the service box each team is then allowed to let the ball bounce on their side one more time. If the ball bounces a second time they lose the point. All other normal rules apply. You will be amazed by: 1. How many balls bounce that could easily be taken out of the air, and 2. How much more urgently players move to get to a ball to save a bounce after they have lost a few points.

No Bounce Doubles - It's nearly always a good idea to start with one bounce doubles with any doubles team, and then when they begin to do very well, allow advanced players to play No Bounce Doubles, which means after the serve the ball cannot bounce at all. One of my very best doubles teams which went 42-2 over two seasons was quite good at this. That same team was undefeated in post season play.

Best Two of Three - 60% of games are won by the player who wins the first point, and 80% of games are won by the player who first gets to 30 in the game. Playing best Two of Three helps players to start games very well.

Start at 30-40 or 40-30 - Playing a set where the score is 30-40 or 40-30 can create numerous scenarios, mainly along the lines of finishing games well. You can start equal level players in either scenario, or you can put a superior player in a 30-40 hole in every game against a weaker opponent.

Tiebreakers with Dice or Playing Cards - Take out some playing cards or dice and use only ace to 5. Dice will allow for a 6 to be rolled, you could decide that 6 means 5. Each player picks a card, and that is the beginning score of a Tiebreaker.

Kamikaze Doubles - Players play doubles with one special rule, if the server's net person makes contact with the return of serve, their team does not lose the point. Additionally, you may need to institute a rule where the net person must make a full effort for every return. Your net player will learn their true range at the net and might be surprised at how far out it is from their original starting position. You may need to adjust some player's initial starting position into the very center of the service box to allow them to get over to cover the middle. With coachable players you can have the discussion about when they start to make errors by trying to go too far. I also emphasize that the server should not switch behind their opponent unless a. The net person crosses the center line, and b. The net person has made the volley. As soon as they are sure the ball will not get through the net person, they can make the switch. Players must not lob the return.

Doubles First Shot must be Lob - Lobbed returns can be deadly for or against you, when you play a full sets or tiebreakers where returners must lob, it really hones the skills of the serving team to hit overheads on the next shot.

Doubles Big Rectangle is Out - When you play this way, the premium is on keeping the ball low, and not relying so much of speed of shot, the alleys are still good, so there is an avenue up the line for a ball on the outside.

Singles Down the Line Gambit - If you are the first player to hit down the line, but you don't win the point on your very next shot, then the opponent gets three points. But if you do go down the line and win the point on a winner or the next shot then you get two points.

Timed Cross Court Execution - from Paul Wardlaw's 'Pressure

Tennis', give your players 5 minutes and see how many times they can serve and make 4 consecutive crosscourt shots starting with the return. You can make it a competition between courts. Also you can add bonus points for longer rallies. Depending on the level of your team you can lengthen or shorten the time to create greater confidence or challenge.

CHAPTER TWENTY-TWO
Team Building

The above process may take two or three weeks to complete, but when done your players will be competent at the new tactic.

Your team captains are the ones most likely to maintain unity of purpose. When they do a great job of this, your job is much easier. If they themselves are divisive, then you have to be more proactive in breaking down divisions, and it will be much more difficult. I love a section from Jim Loehr's book, *Mental Toughness Training for Sports*. He lists the following as things that can bring unity or division to the team:

1. Get to know your teammates.

2. Give your teammates positive feedback.

3. Give 100% effort in practice, work on your weakness.

4. Realize that positivism and negativism are contagious and there are no neutrals.

5. Resolve conflicts with coaches or teammates as quickly as possible.

6. Get your attitude and disposition right before going to practice or

games.

7. Let your racket do the talking.

8. Go out of your way to help teammates or coaches whenever you can.

9. Be fully responsible for yourself; don't make excuses.

10. Be your own best igniter.

11. Communicate clearly, honestly, and openly with your coach.

12. Have fun, and do your best to make it fun for everyone.

I have players select the one thing they can do that is an area of strength to operate in, and do that for our team. The whole list can be overwhelming. I read it a few times and include it in our season packet at the beginning. I also ask them to identify an area of weakness and work on that. My experience is that 100% effort and negativity are the two chief problems on any given team, but it varies by school. Different school cultures bring different sets of problems, but this list captures most all of them.

CHAPTER TWENTY-THREE
Motivation, Rewards and Humility

As much as we like to think that our players are very intrinsically motivated and won't need any kind of tangible award, we have to remember that everyone has a little kid in them and prizes are fun. Giving tangible awards give a concrete reminder of something that happened. Over the years I have had teams that really needed awards, and other years I have teams where it seemed only one or two players may ever be deserving of the award.

Player of the Month - Players of the month are mostly awarded for big wins, but there can also be other factors involved like behaviors that helped the team in a big way. Each player of the month should also then be a candidate for Most Valuable, Most Improved, Most Inspirational.

Fastest off the Court - When my team is the favorite, we play a game where the first player to come off with a win and at least one 6-0 set, gets an overgrip. If a player then finishes later, but wins 6-0,6-0, that player surges into first place. Up to three players can get an overgrip for winning a set 6-0. One very important rule: They must never show to their opponent that they are in a hurry, and they must never talk about what they did until the next day at practice. This potentially can be seen as disrespectful of the opponent, but really I use it as a tool to help players maintain focus. This little motivational tool helps players to think about winning every game, instead of letting a game or two slip away from their grasp. Also, everyone wins, because the matches ends sooner and everyone can go home to do homework.

45 minute rule - This one requires a good relationship with players, so that they understand the meaning of staying on the court. Sometimes you know a player at a certain position is overmatched. And in the context of team play, if one of the players loses a very fast match, the players who play on neighboring courts sense that and it does not give them confidence. Even in a potential 6-0, 6-0 loss, I tell my players that I want them to stay on the court for at least 45 minutes. I have seen high school sets last 11 minutes, so we certainly want to avoid a match that lasts under 30 minutes on our end. The player should fight for every point. Every single point you win can add 30 seconds to the match. Take the full time allotted between points without stalling, to think about if there is a certain shot that gives the player a little more trouble than the others. I will sometimes tell a player if we have a strong relationship, "If you come off the court in under 45 minutes, don't talk to me after", then wink at them. When they succeed its important to praise them for their efforts. Sometimes the opponent can become impatient and it can effect their play, then your player wins a few games.

Not Noticing When They Miss - Maybe one the coolest things I learned to do is when my players make a bad error. It's amazing the high percentage of times a player will make an error, then they will look around to see who saw them miss. Mostly, they will look for the coach. If at that moment we give them a disapproving look, they know two things, you saw them, and you did not like it. How long will that thought plague their young mind? Longer for kids with less mental strength, shorter for those with more. What I do is the moment I see an error from my player, I quickly turn and busy myself. Quite often I catch a glimpse of my player looking relieved that I did not see it. Players can feel the positivity or negativity coming from outside the fences.

The Post Match Talk - How and who you talk about is very important. As much as possible keep it brief and positive. In 27 years I can count on one hand the times I have taken my team to task over a loss or a poor performance. So find the positives, talk about them and do your best to find something to say nicely about different players. Many times its best to save the analysis of what happened for the next day. Young people love to be praised in front of their peers.

Honor Opponents - No matter what motivational tricks you use with your team, it's best if the other team has no idea what you are doing. My teams have been on the other end of this, when players seemed to be racing on court in order to win the fastest match contest. Once, there was a time that I had heard that money was involved, that also seems to be a bad idea. Players must not rush off the court, they must give a good handshake, thank the opponent for the match, and walk off the court with opponent.

Why do this? The immediacy and the limited nature of these rewards make them highly motivating for many players. Some players won't care about the reward, but they will take note that in a match you can win easily, its best to get it over sooner, rather than later.

Mercy - The most merciful thing you can do as the heavy favorite is to end the match as quickly as possible. I have seen teams that give a patronizing message of 'We will play nice with you', or 'We will toy with you'. Some of the worst interactions I have had with other coaches were when the opponent would play with their non-dominant hand, 'drop-shot lob' the whole match, or carry on a conversation with fans or other players during the match. As educators, its our duty to create an atmosphere of mutual respect.

Focus and Concentration - Where a player may become bored when leading 4-love or 5-love, if they have a carrot dangling in front of them, they can keep their motivation even if they go down in the game. Under normal circumstances a player who is down 30-love on the opponent's serve may just play down for a couple points to prepare for their own serve. The opponent may also ramp up their effort level. Perhaps the opponent's lack of effort at the beginning was the reason for the deficit. Having a small motivational piece can also help a player to thwart the opponents last ditch effort to save the set.

Save Time and Energy - The big picture of all of this is that when the match is shorter, players go home sooner. They use less overall energy over the course of a season, and they will be more fresh for the post season.

CHAPTER TWENTY-FOUR
Threat Assessment

Jeff Greenwald recently gave a presentation about the developing brains of teenagers. He stated that research seems to indicate that most teenagers have fully developed abilities to detect a threat and respond to a threat, that they perceive. They can perceive threats visually, aurally or from other senses. What is not fully developed in many of their brains is their cerebral cortex which is in charge of regulating the response to threats. The coach or other adults are best advised to be a source of help, so that players can make more synaptic connections, realizing that some things are not a threat.

Generally, I notice that if one of my players has made what they think is a bad or otherwise embarrassing error, the first thing they do is look for me. Many times they want to know if I saw their mistake. I have learned to quickly look away and pretend to be busy with something else. When I look back I get a sense that they are relieved because they thought that I did not see their mistake. As our relationship improves and we can talk more and more about their strengths and weaknesses, then they don't see me as a threat, but a help, and that I am not on the outside of the court judging them constantly.

Recently in a league final match a player who is concerned about her reputation hesitated to call for a lines person. I helped her to realize that it was not because we distrust the other player's integrity, we just thought her eyes were letting her down because of the moment. Later, my player began to play some out balls, because she was worried that the lines person might think she was cheating if she made a close call. Casually in the midst of some on court coaching I stated, "I trust that you make good calls, trust yourself too, call it out if it's out. If you make a mistake, the lines people are here to help, so don't worry." It seemed to help her to know that she did not need to play out balls. From what I could tell, her calls were flawless, and unfortunately we noticed that the other player was calling some in balls out, and also playing some obvious out balls as good. This confirmed our thought that the big moment had her at a high anxiety level.

In the story about the player with a groin pull, I'm pretty certain that the player sensed a threat from me. Not knowing my level of care about my athletes, and my balanced holistic approach to their long term health over short term achievements, I think he assumed that if I knew he was hurt, that I would pull him from the lineup. Another possibility is that I might not acknowledge the injury and drive him hard to win. Instead, I quickly accepted the situation that he told me about his injury after losing a set and being down a break. From that point we worked together to develop a strategy that would require less movement from him. Also, I made it quite clear that if he experienced more pain, that he would let me know and he would stop his match in order to save the rest of his season. He nursed that injury for most of the rest of the season, and he did regain full health in a few weeks. That also meant that I held him out of some conditioning during practice.

The above interactions send a message to the rest of the team as well, and you can gain the trust of your team. Once they don't see the coach as a threat, then player and coach can work together to reduce the sense of threat from other situations that would seem to pose a greater threat.

CHAPTER TWENTY-FIVE
Road Trips, Dinners and Events

Now that you have some ideas for how to build team chemistry, now you need to get your team together outside of a match or practice. One of my favorite activities with a team is to take them overnight to a tournament, get hotel rooms, and play two full days. This leads to many meals together, and the bonding experience of going to a strange new place. Sharing a room together and eating can bring a team very closely together.

At different times, my teams have been the ones to initiate having a team dinner at a restaurant, other teams I know of host them at the home of one of the players.

Wayne Bryan, perhaps the greatest 'pied piper' for tennis in the USA, travels the country to talk to coaches and tennis teaching professionals. He urges coaches to take their players to see professional and collegiate tennis. This can be an eye opening experience for your team.

Based on Wayne's urging, I took kids to our local ATP event which every time was a tremendous boost in excitement and motivation for the players. The greatest part of a trip like that is when a few players are really struck by the tennis bug and really ramp up their efforts to play and improve.

Another great idea is to attend other sporting events at the school. Football games, or basketball games can be a very exciting event to attend. Also, when you show up as a team, you send a strong message to the greater school culture that you care about the overall athletic program, and you gain some capital in that way.

It can't be said enough do things outside of matches and practices and your team will grow together.

CHAPTER TWENTY-SIX
Who Gains from High School Tennis?

"My Name is Mike Eruzione and I play for the United States of America"
~ Miracle a film about the 1980 US Men's Hockey Olympic Gold Medal
Performance

There is no 'I' in team, but there is a "ME", all you have to do is tear apart
team to make it. Let's start there. People make the assumption that
because tennis is essentially an individual sport you can add or remove a
player to the team and make the team instantly better or worse, and that
a better player added to the team makes the overall experience better.
Conversely, remove that player from the team and it gets worse. In the
overall scheme of things for the high school experience of the players at
the school, this is false. Sometimes adding a talented but selfish player
can wreck everything, sometimes their removal can create some early
adversity, but long term gains.

Tennis teams are in fact teams. A team is a united group who all seek to
go toward the same goals. There are many great reasons for a player to
decide to play high school tennis, and a few valid reasons why they
should avoid it. There are also some great guidelines about how to
approach the program.

Join the Team:

1. To be a part of something bigger than yourself. Regardless of outcomes, this alone is a key factor in your future success as a human being

2. If you are a tremendous player, then it would be wise to give back to the sport. Giving back is a much more meaningful expression of gratitude than simply saying thank you. Thankfulness being that which you give voice to, and gratitude being the actions you take to support your words. Some claim to love the game, but then fail to contribute where it can matter the most.

3. To have a path similar to the vast majority of professional athletes who played high school sports even though they had a private coach teaching them to hit, or be a quarterback or shoot a basketball. The great majority of professional team athletes may have played for less-talented coaches than their private coach. In most sports, the high school coach is quite accomplished and garners wide respect.

4. To be an ambassador for the sport and your school. Take pride in your neighborhood and your school.

Poor Reasons NOT to Join:

1. It's all about *you.*

2. *You* have nothing to gain from it, or so it seems.

3. *Your* time is too valuable and you can't afford to waste a minute of it. As though your time is more valuable than other people's time.

4. USTA ranking points are the only way *you* can be considered to be a pro or college player (in *your* mind). In reality ratings are having a growing influence in recruitment, and there are some great ways to get recruited that don't have a lot to do with a ranking.

5. *You* will grudgingly play, but only if given special treatment by

the coach to pursue better coaching, as though you have the power to negotiate.

Ask yourself, do you want to be on a team, or do you want the team to be about *you*? I have seen and heard of many future professional athletes who were men or women among boys and girls in the high school arena of play, yet they played.

My vision of high school tennis, is that elite tennis players could participate and be an inspiration to younger players at their school, creating a better environment moving forward. More good players would play, schools would be forced to hire better coaches, and more talent would be discovered because a freshman kid would get a chance to admire a top-flight competitor deciding then to work hard for four years to play college tennis. But I guess if you are only thinking of what you want right now, then you don't see yourself as part of the health of American tennis, then that is sad and unfortunate for everyone.

Here are a few different scenarios that may help guide your decision whether to play for your team, along with some helpful hints on how to make it work.

1. If you are very best player at the school, and not one player on the team can hit two balls in a row against you, ask the coach to find out what can be done. Defer to the coach! Don't threaten or cajole. Express your desire to play on the team in a way that works for everyone. Let him or her decide if it's worth it for the whole team. It could mean coming to practice, helping teach the lesser kids, or playing only the matches. If a workable solution can be made, then make it. If not, don't play.

2. You are the best player, but there are enough good players on the team that can at least give you a workout. Portions of practice are designed to help you get your workout. Maybe your private coach and the head coach can confer. Make this work the best you can. Also realize that not 100% of practice will go your way. Help the

players on your team get to your level.

3. You are not the best player on the team, but the coach is not as knowledgeable as you would prefer. Ask about working with the top players, and let the coach know that you are very interested in improving. Is there any flexibility to work with a private coach during the week?

4. Some coaches have a built-in day to work with private coaches. Fridays are most common. Although I have never done that, I can see how it works for some, and it fueled a few notable exceptions I made and those are captured in the stories below.

5. You don't play. Everyone on the team knows you could dramatically help the team, but you don't. The second best player at the school becomes MVP, but never really feels like he or she deserved it, because if you played you would have been MVP. The school does not acknowledge you, and your results do not appear in the newspaper. At high school reunions you will be the one that was not on the team. You will not have inspired anyone who was on the team, because you held yourself separate from them.

CHAPTER TWENTY-SEVEN
Team Selection System

It's very important to have your team selection system set and in place prior to any meetings. I have made a few mistakes in team selection that dearly cost me credibility with players, parents and administration. Consider carefully how you select the team, because it will reflect your values as a coach. One large part of the goal for team selection is team unity. I let players know that the criteria for selection to the team revolve around their playing ability, but attitude, work ethic, team player mentality, athletic ability, and best fit for the program moving forward are also nearly equal. I also stress that I look at their ability to win matches, not simply if they have nice strokes.

Every team has a player who wins at a level that is higher than his or her technical proficiency, and another player who does not win as much as their technique would indicate. In the meeting I will even say, "While of course I look at results, I also look at these other factors, and it's quite possible--in fact, it seems to happen in most years--that someone may assume they will make the team because they beat a certain player. In fact, if you are a junior or a senior, and you are not well inside the top 18 players on the team, you most likely will not make the squad because that spot is best taken by a freshman."

When I coach last-place teams, I take anyone who wants to play. They usually cut themselves from the team once we get to work. That's ok, because sadly they are being honest about how much effort they want to put into their game. When you are making your system, consider all factors. How many courts do you have? At what point in your ladder is their a large drop off in playing ability? When is there a significant drop off? Do you want "ne'er do wells?" How much time do you have to spend with beginners? Do you have a full squad? Can you tolerate one disruptive player and have your captains help you get them to buy into what you are doing? Does your selection process promote excellence?

No-Cut Coach

I think I may have been a no-cut coach at one point, but I suppose the player's cut themselves. I am curious about the experiences of dedicated no-cut coaches and what the positive and negative aspects are in a program like that. If you are doing it because you are desperate for big numbers, that could be a problem. I took over a program where the chief complaint from players was that he previous coach kept 50% more players than I did, which lead to reduced and ill managed court time. By no means was my team extremely small, but we did manage to keep everyone playing on court 95% of the time.

To what extant can there be behavior problems with too large of a squad? This is for you the coach to decide.

CHAPTER TWENTY-EIGHT
Learn from 25 years of Mistakes

My first year of coaching a girls team, I allowed myself to be swayed by the way the team had operated at the school in previous years. When taking over a new team it's important to acknowledge and communicate that the program will be different. I advise that its a great idea to change something about the program intentionally to put your stamp on the team moving forward. "Yes, I know that in past years you did it that way, but now we do it this way.". This team had always had singles challenge matches even for doubles spots on the team. I did not know my team very well, and only later did I realize that there was subtle intimidation being directed at the player from the wrong side of the tracks, in favor of the player who was not quite as good but who had many friends on the team. I realized far too late what was happening and I was also ill equipped to deal with the bigotry over social status on that team.

Back then I used only results as my criteria, which did not allow me to make a decision in regard to any other factors, as stated in the earlier chapter on team selection. The girl who won that challenge match to join the team, later would prove not to have much in the way of work ethic, but with the aid of some intimidation, beat the girl that was humble and hard working. The humble girl, by virtue of her deferential nature, did not assert herself nor complain, as she most likely felt intimidated about not being wanted by the team at large. I have always felt bad about that. The girl that stayed dragged down players above her with her lack of practice ability. The other girl would have been a great motivator as a "shark in the water." The good news is that our girl from the wrong side the tracks, took a lot of lessons, came back strong, and played varsity as a sophomore.

Another time, I had a player who always seemed to talk back, and when I told him that new players need to be a bit more quiet until they get up to speed with the program, he smirked and made another comment. My future self would cut him right there and then, but wait until after the day to inform him. As it turned out, that player was a major cancer on the team. He lacked the backbone to compete, complained about the workouts, and dragged down his doubles partner with criticism. In those years, players purchased their uniforms and kept them after the season. I hounded this player all season who never paid for his uniform. At the end of the season, he brought the uniform back to me so as to resolve himself of the responsibility. I refused. "You own it now, even though you never paid for it." I am happy to say he did not return the next year. But that season was one of the most underachieving seasons, largely due to the distractions and discouragement of one player. It was a difficult season for the team. Perhaps it would have been much better for everyone if that player had been cut. We will never know. I still did not have a strong criteria established for team selection that would have allowed me not to select him, and would make for a better season. I fielded many complaints from players that year about his behavior during practice, and his teammates gave him a rather derogatory nickname, which led to some conflict as well. The disruption to our work ethic as a team due to one player resulted in a lower spot in the standings than what I thought we were capable of achieving. Of all the factors for success or failure, this one disruptive player was most likely the number one factor in our outcome.

I have also made the mistake of underestimating certain players. I sometimes get dazzled by big serves, forehands, or imposing specimens, discounting players with simple strokes, but outstanding instincts, iron will, and great concentration.

AW joined the team as a sophomore, and I found out later he had played a lot of basketball. A very gifted athlete, although smaller in stature, he slowly crept up the JV ladder as he learned how to play tennis. I must admit, I had a very large team, and I was just one coach, so I did not watch every JV match as closely as I could. I realized that it was near the end of the season, and I had only seen glimpses of AW playing, and frankly was never impressed.

In our final match of the season, I watched and was amazed. With fairly tight and somewhat robotic strokes, AW could put the ball anywhere he wanted on the court. He also used shot combinations quite often. He showed that understood the court from a tactical sense. At that moment, I realized I had missed an opportunity to train him more intentionally.

The next year he became a strong varsity contributor. Having played #2 doubles in his junior year, I challenged him to play on my summer team. We had an A team made up of our top players and those from other teams in our league, and a B team, which was all of our teams players the next rung down. Opting to playing #1 singles on the B team was asking for a summer of torture. AW took on that role, returned his senior year as our team captain, played #2 singles, and went 15-1. He was the heartbeat of a team that surprisingly tied for a championship in a year I thought we might finish fourth, or possibly third if we pulled some upsets.

Now on to another story of a player who was overlooked. On the first day of tryouts at the very beginning of a new season, I like to get all the new players trying out for the team in a singles round robin, and then a doubles mixer. On one team we had a group of 12 new players out of 55 trying out for 24 spots. I knew I had to quickly eliminate a large group of players, or tryouts would drag on for a lengthy period.

T was in this group. Within a very short while of watching these players, it was obvious that 11 out of 12 were not going to make it. T did. His game was not at all remarkable to look at. In the next segment, he did fairly poorly, and just barely made the next cut. I took him aside and let him know that I thought he played tennis well enough to perhaps make the team, but he should relax and just perform. Each stage he made it through, but never really distinguished himself. His smooth game lacked power, with not a lot of excess motion in his strokes, good volleyer, nice game.

As the season progressed, I lost track of T during a fairly tough season of establishing my philosophy with a team of kids who were trained at various academies. T was on the JV team, and I did not see him play much except in large group games. During that season, I had quite a bit of frustration with another player on the varsity who was wildly talented with a big forehand and laser serve (when he chose to hit it, and hit it in), but for various reasons did not play well when it mattered the most. When voicing my frustration, my JV coach said, "You should give T a try." I said, "I am not convinced that he has enough game to succeed at the varsity level."

Eventually the frustration with the so-called talented player reached a peak when he dragged his doubles partner down one more time, this time in a winnable first round playoff match. It was over! I had decided to pull him from the lineup, especially against the #1 seeded team in the next round. I gave T another look, inserted him in that doubles team, and developed what chemistry we could. I figured that since we did not have a great chance to beat the #1 seeded team in the section playoffs as a 9th seed, it would be great for the future of the team to have two freshmen playing #3 doubles, T being one of those. T and C (another player) played out of their minds and beat two seniors in what was the pivotal match in our upset of the #1 seeds. This story is about the mistake of not continuing to assess the players improvement through the season so as to select them. Pay attention to the improvement of every player, and listen to your assistant! I always heard her, but the fact that T backed it up with better and better play, allowed me to act on what she was saying. Thank you Coach Ellen.

CHAPTER TWENTY-NINE
Challenge Matches

I have a very simple philosophy about challenge matches: The coach directs it. Why? I am more a believer in team unity and familiarity with your position, than I am of a team in constant competition with one another.

I run challenges in a very measured way until about two weeks before the regular season, but I may go another week if there are some very close matches. All the challenges then fit into my practice schedule. First, I take the top players who have a legitimate shot of being singles starters, and I have them play a round robin of 10-point tie-breakers. From there, an order is established, and then it becomes like the finals of a bowling tournament: 7 plays 6, winner plays 5, winner plays 4, and so on. It very easily aligns the team.

Of course, as a coach you can look for a bad performance and wonder if the player deserves a second chance. When coaches are not proactive and/or paying attention, then some inequities can exist in the lineup, and some team members can become discontent. I let everyone know that if a player has improved a lot, we will have a mid-season challenge match. In my later years of coaching, I have only had a handful of mid-season challenge matches. The players accept it because they understand that all our competition is best focused outward onto our opponents.

They would never say it, but it allows them to cope with knowing where they stand on the team.

Simultaneously with Once I know who is left out of singles, I get to work on pairing up doubles teams. For this, I take four players and have them play A and B vs. C and D, A and C vs. B and D, and A and D vs. B and C. They play tie-breakers, and we record the cumulative point scores. In the top flight the top three stay, and fourth place drops into the next flight. In flight two, the top player moves to top flight, and then the last place player moves to flight three. I do this for a number of rounds, and its interesting to see the cream rise to the top.

A few interesting things happen, and some surprising chemistry is discovered. You will see in points that these two do extremely well together, so when the final teams are set, perhaps those two stay together. This method also helps the players to see themselves as doubles players who can succeed on a doubles court with any partner. You may also see a player who got unlucky or missed a crucial shot, and they head into a tailspin.

I remember one top player falling three flights in a row. We later talked about this because he was in despair. I reassured him that I knew he would be in the running for a varsity spot and not to worry. The next day he moved right back up. For the sake of keeping things even, longer tie-breakers like a 9-7 result are recorded as 7-5.

CHAPTER THIRTY
Team and Parent Meetings

For your first team meeting of the season, plan the meeting to be brief, create a buzz, and concisely outline your goals and expectations. I find that a great meeting can save a lot of time and energy later, and some young people may or may not decide not to try out based on your expectations. Others will be inspired because now there are higher expectations. If you give out a hand out to players they have something to read and refer to later.

Your school most likely has a requirement of holding a parent meeting, either with players or not. These can be very important, but I will share about a time when the meeting did not matter at all. Realize that sharing honestly with parents what you expect of players, and who you are as a coach gives them the understanding of what kinds of things they may hear from their student.

Daily Meetings

When having regular meetings with players that last 5 to 10 minutes or when teaching a strategy or skill, I like to have the players stand in a circle. I do this for three reasons:

    1. No one can hide behind anyone else and all players can see every

other player.

2. The circle is the most unified shape. Symbolic unity is created.

3. The players will have a higher degree of attentiveness.

When going over details for the week, I like to have the upperclassmen state what the schedule is for the week, then have the freshmen parrot back certain details of the message. It's remarkable how preoccupied the mind of a freshman in high school can be.

A brief meeting at every practice is a great time to reflect on great play the day before, focus on an area the team needs to improve, and be sure everyone knows the schedule for the week. Many times, practical issues have been discovered and solved by the group because they were paying attention to a detail that escaped my attention. Players should be empowered to engage in discussion. However, I strongly discourage lower class men, from gaining their information from other lower class men. Everyone is encouraged to talk with captains. Captains are expected to give accurate information to anyone who asks.

If you have a short meeting just after the warm-up period and another at the end of practice to catch any details missed, you will have a much more organized group of players.

CHAPTER THIRTY-ONE
Days One through Three

Set the Tone

Explain the rules, stick to the rules, and use wisdom. Establish a disciplined approach early on, and there is hope that you can have a fun season.

If you want to have a season that is not very fun, then make sure you have a lot of rules. Too many rules will turn you into 'coach-cop'. Instead, come up with three to five rules that really make a difference with the type of experience players will have on the team. Establish targeted consequences aimed at achieving a goal with the team and specific players. Do not punish the whole team for the infraction of one or a small group of people. (When did that ever become a popular idea?) Explaining the reason for the rules is helpful, such as, "I want everyone to be here on time because we get more done in less time, and improve 5 to 10% better, and you also feel better about yourself if you come early." Here are some things to consider:.

1. Practice starts on time, and ends on time. Those that come late or leave early without prior arrangement are subject to consequences.

2. Respect everyone and their possessions. Small amounts of

disrespect can be the match that starts a forest fire. Blow out the match. One thing that has always bothered me is the secret disrespect of one player to another. Hidden and out of view, it was nothing I could see. If that player had come to me and trusted me, I would wisely draw out the situation and solve it. Solving the problem of open disrespect should start the very first time it happens. This creates a safer and more secure environment.

3. Give 100% effort at all times. I don't know who the moron was that started saying it is possible to give 110%, because how can you give more than you have? Players trying to do that get hurt, burned out, and feel quite a bit of anxiety. Besides most teenagers don't feel the difference between 95% and 100%. So be sure to accept quality over quantity. Sometimes I will say, "I did not see 100% effort on that footwork drill, so here is an extra one. Let me know if you want to continue to have quantity over quality. I prefer quality over quantity. If every player gives 100% effort this time, then we are done with this exercise." It is far more valuable to show players when they have given less than 100% effort.

4. Communication must be done by the player to the coach. Grow up, and don't have your mom call unless you are extremely sick. Never have your friend deliver a message to me for you. Can you be certain they even will? In the modern age of communication, I have come to accept that some amount of text messaging is a convenient way to communicate.

5. Players must be on court practicing 30 minutes prior to the start of the match. This one rule has had a significant impact on helping players get off to a good start. When warming up, I want the players to spend 10 minutes on groundstrokes, 5 minutes on serves, and when there is 5 minutes left before I call them in for our talk, I say exactly these words. "Okay, (team name), let's hit some serves." Having your players serve for 5 full minutes gives them the best opportunity to get loose prior to the match.

6. Every player must stay while the Varsity match is still in progress.

Why do tennis players think its okay to leave a match in progress because they did their part? I do occasionally make exceptions, but only with responsible players who make a prior arrangement and not in a situation where it could have been planned better.

Those are some sample rules, but I also let them know that the rules of the school also apply, so that saves me from making up a lot of new ones. Listed 6 here, but you can add or subtract. Boiling the rules down to three that matter to your team, is a great idea.

CHAPTER THIRTY-TWO
Breaking Down "The Mantra"

In pre-season meetings, I like to teach the players about realistic goals. I owe a debt to Jim Loehr for this, although I have adapted the goals and changed them to suit me and my teams. Jim wrote about realistic versus unrealistic goal-setting in the book he co-authored with Jack Groppel and Pat Etcheberry, *The Science of Coaching Tennis*. Teenagers are notorious for having unrealistic expectations, and we can help them get grounded in better goals. The following goals are process oriented, rather than outcome oriented. Winning is obvious, process is not.

The mantra that we recite prior to matches goes like this: "Today, confidence is my biggest weapon. I will give 100% effort, enjoy the competition, and show myself as strong and wise. I learn from every match. I get 65% of my first serves in play, my feet in position for every shot, and continually pressure my opponent. I love a tough match."

Goal #1: Give 100% Effort. Effort level is one of the main cornerstones upon which our mental games are built. If a player can become self aware enough to notice small differences in effort level and get it right back to work then, that shows a lot of maturity on their part. If that player can get back on track for the next point or even on the next shot, then they protect themselves from poor play. Also, there is a message that is sent to the opponent: "I never take a point off. You will have to work for every point." When one player is giving 100% effort and the other 95% effort or less, that can be the decisive factor in the match. Lesser players can beat better players who are in cruise control. Once a player accepts 97% effort, then they may not notice when it slips to 95% or below. Players must learn to manage their own energy and effort level to avoid ending up "in the tank."

Additionally, there is an issue of respect that goes along with 100% effort. Players feel better about themselves when they give a more thorough effort throughout the match. Self-respect is protected when you get to the end of a tough match, and you can acknowledge that you gave your best effort. You also respect your opponent when you are the heavy favorite, while giving your best effort. This issue is also fundamental to the lowest level of mental toughness, the one where players don't give 100% effort because they fear the responsibility of having to always do that. They then can have a handy excuse for losing. Player's who have excuses for losing protect themselves from learning the real lessons of how to compete to win. These immature players may even say, "I would have beaten you if I had tried."

Sometimes 'tanking', the lack of giving 100% effort, occurs in practice. When I work with players to help them learn new shots or tactics, I see a range of enthusiasm in working with the change. Periodically players may go in the tank with regard to their attempts at the shot or the tactic, then immediately turn and say, "See, it didn't work!". That's when I say, "*You* didn't work!" Sometimes I hear kids say, "This drill doesn't work." My response is, "Drills don't work, people do! Make that drill work." Each instance of this kind of tanking is unique and each coach will need to discover with that player how they can get the player to give 100% effort in the learning of new techniques or tactics.

Goal #2: Enjoy the Competition. "Competere" is Latin for "two seeking together," so all competition has an element of cooperation to play by certain rules to have fair competition. It's meant to be friendly. In my experience, boys usually enjoy competition more than girls. Competition brings with it a thrill. There is a strong visceral excitement that comes from playing an opponent that you don't know, or that you don't see often. Learning to compete from the beginning to the end is one of the important life lessons found in sports, that carries forward into real life situations.

Goal #3 Show myself Strong and Wise. Players show strength with great body language, eye contact, speaking clearly--these outward signs show confidence. The wisdom of how to deal with the match, opponent, and competition with poise also develops strong life skills as well. Players will need to learn how to proactively deal with bad calls, sportsmanship and show wisdom when playing for their team.

Goal #4 Learn from Every Match. It has been said "Sometimes you win and sometimes you learn", but I don't think that is the best possible statement. I want my players to learn in every match regardless of the outcome. We state this before every match, that we will learn something. If players believe that winning means they don't have to learn anything, then they lose out on the experience of discovering what they can do better even after winning. Another issue I have with philosophy that losing produces more learning than winning is that it can be philosophical crutch for players to lean on to excuse losing. The object of any game is to win, and committing fully to learning about the process of improvement improves your chances of favorable outcomes over time! If you fail at the top three goals above, but achieve goal #4 then your match was not a total loss.

When you, players on your team or the entire team achieve all four goals, then you will have your best chance of winning the match. Even if you don't win the match you will find that players will gain some satisfaction from having achieved their pre-match goals. This is especially motivating for teams that are not vying for championships, but simply want to become more competitive in their league or local rivalry.

CHAPTER THIRTY-THREE
Managing Injuries

"The #1 factor that keeps athletes from improving is injury." ~*John Jerome*

Managing Injuries When it comes to injuries, the stakes can be very high. Our players longterm health and well-being are at risk. The stakes increase when injuries are mismanaged. Not often do high school tennis coaches work with the athletic trainer at the school. When I was at a school with a trainer, I worked hard to develop a strong relationship, so that we would understand each other and the needs of athletes. The trainer usually only works with 'real' athletes. Tennis, perhaps, requires more athleticism than any other sport, however tennis athletes tend to be the most undertrained for their sport. Furthermore, issue of injury management is made more complicated by the fears that young players have until their coach shows that he cares more about their long-term health and full season participation than today's conditioning or an early season match.

Express Care and Concern When you go out of your way as a coach to express that you are most interested in the long term health and welfare of the players, they may begin to trust you more. Conversely, some players will want to disregard their own health for the benefit of the team. There will be some circumstances in which a player may want to play hurt, and/or the coach may ask the player to play in an important contest for the team. The decision to play hurt must be weighed carefully, especially if there is a risk of further injury. Very rarely have I asked a player to perform while hurt, but have always told them "If if feels any worse, then you can end the match at any time. A handful of times, players have had to stop, more often my players have continued to play and sometimes quite heroically. Be sure to let players know you want to know if they have an injury or even if they are extremely sore and worn down.

Chronic or Overuse Injuries When a chronic injury develops, there is usually something about the training or the habits of the player that causes this to happen. There could be something about practice that is contributing to the problem if more than one player develops this. When is it best to respond? After two players complain? Five? Twenty? If I hear from two or more players that they are starting to feel a tight or sore shoulder then I will begin to talk to other players on the team to find out how their shoulders feel. If we are in the middle of serving at that time I might shorten the serving practice session. Over the course of the next few days or weeks I would check in with my players about their shoulders. It may seem odd, but teenagers really do suffer in silence much of the time. I have discovered that a few players express having shoulder soreness more often then not many players on the team feel the same.

Acute Injuries One of my very best players was playing a match against his top rival and lost the first set 6-0. Having won less than 10 points, he wasn't moving well and looked upset. He told me during the match that he had been nursing a slightly pulled groin, but felt like he had aggravated it in the warm up.

We were in the midst of a major match against our main league rivals. In the middle of that moment is not the time to open up the emotional can of worms, we figured out how he was going to play to reduce the pressure on the groin. I gave him permission to retire from the match at any time, and said he should not make any sudden cuts for the ball. He might have to let a shot or two go. The great news is that he managed to come back from 6-1, 4-0 to win 1-6, 7-6, 6-2. He was able to avoid hurting himself worse, and we also forged a bond of trust whereby he knew he could tell me if he was not not 100% healthy.

Players sometimes fear they will be thought to be weak, lose playing time, lose their position, because coaches may overreact to their health concerns. The players might not be in touch with what their body is trying to tell them. Others still may try to be brave, ignore and push past their pain and end up with a severe injury. We all know that there is another subgroup of players who may whine about minor aches and pains, so always engage those minor complaints with care and reassurance. It is far better to engage and show concern with sincerity about every ache and pain, real or imagined.

"Sorry to hear that, but it doesn't seem like its too much to worry about. Let me know if it feels any worse. Get some ice on it. After practice you can always see the trainer." I have had a very small number of players who had 'phantom' injuries; and it is not the norm. Most youngsters will try to keep their pain secret, and only consistent trust building with you will give them freedom to tell you how they feel.

A common scenario is that you notice a player is experiencing a drop off in their velocity, accuracy or spin on their serve. You address it technically, but you don't know the player feels tight. Compounding the problem mentally and emotionally for the player by adding something to think about in terms of technique can put a load on the player and be a major factor for diminished results. I have learned to start with, "How are you? It looks like your serve has lost effectiveness, do you know why?" He might say, "Yes, Coach, my shoulder is very sore." At that point you may then discover which serve most affects it and then eliminate that serve for that match. Perhaps the focus could be more on placement rather than speed or spin, and you can make up for that by being ready to return some tougher balls on the first shot. Now the player can feel free to shift the game play, not hurt themselves worse, and feel a bit more confident about today's outcome.

CHAPTER THIRTY-FOUR
Injury Stories

K had an exotic upper body connective tissue injury which made his pec feel weak on his dominant side. He sought out every form of treatment you might try, but he found no relief. I asked the team to do 40 push-ups, 4 sets by 10. K protested, "I can't do that. You know I'm hurt" I told him "It's a test. If you can't do at least 10 push-ups, then you should not be playing tennis. But please, only do 10." He grumbled, did them, survived, and then in good conscience I could now play him in the line-up. I also discussed this matter fully with his mother. We kept a close eye on him, and there were times he sat out because the pain was too great. I looked closely at the schedule and had some planned dates for him to rest and recover. K was a strong team player, and due to his injury he played doubles only during his junior year, and when a senior and recovered, he was given the option to play singles, but chose doubles with his friend, and they were an MVP doubles team. Every match, I knew I could pencil in a W next to their names, as they went 24-1 over two seasons, including sectional playoffs. Had we not worked closely together, K would have gone over the edge of injury, and not been available to the team.

B was pretty sick. He did not look great and I knew he was not going to win a tough match on the day, but he was also our #1 player. In our area when your #1 player sits, your entire lineup shifts upward one notch. We were facing a rematch with our rival the second place team, so we did not want to give them a strong chance to beat us. Additionally there is a negative psychological effect on the when they know the #1 is out against tough competition. I asked him if he would play at least one set, see how he felt, and then he could retire after a set. Of course, if he had felt much worse more quickly I could have pulled him from the match. He lost the first set 6-1 and retired from the match. People thought I was mean to insert him in the lineup, but I never really intended for him to finish. We won 6-1 that day, but that could have easily turned into a 4-3 win for the other team with him out, as each of their players matched up very well with the next rung on our ladder. Thanks B, for playing that match!

'A' had a sore knee--patellar tendinitis. She was in pain, but not in any danger of a catastrophic injury. She limped along during a few matches late in the season, and needed to sit on the bench for a match to prepare for the postseason. In our final regular season match, again a rival match, she complained of soreness, and I told her, "You can retire anytime you want, but for now keep trying because you never know what might happen. Keep the points short. ". I knew that sometimes when the opponent sees that you are hurt they then have sympathy and can find ways to lose. That happened in this case. 'A' won a tough three-set match, and felt a strong sense of accomplishment from fighting through that. She then iced and rested for a few matches and came back to no knee soreness prior to some huge wins in the playoffs. She was one of our Freshmen Twin Tigers that were so pivotal to a semi-final playoff appearance, followed by a section championship the next year.

CHAPTER THIRTY-FIVE
Having a Sense of Humor

I am fairly embarrassed by my early coaching, but I do accept that you have to start somewhere. All my life I have wanted to make things fun, but also had been on a search to become a serious person in order to find success. It did not work for me. As a 26-year-old, I had been a part-time assistant at a high school and just breaking into the world of coaching when the head coach left to pursue other interests. I interviewed and got the job. An viola! I was instantly no fun.

The idea that I would be measured by my team's wins and losses, and the grandiose vision of the discipline I would bring to my team, made for mixed results at best. We did succeed in taking care of business against all the teams we should and we truly challenged the perennial champs, but it was not very much fun. I had this idea that we would practice for a full two hours and there would be no talking by the players.

At the same school where I was no fun coaching the boy's, I then became head coach of the girl's team. During a fragile time in the girl's team season, the former coach who was much loved and respected by the girls came by for a visit, at a time when I was really struggling to find a way to guide them. At that time the girls were not completely happy with me, nor I with them. When the beloved former coach came back, the girls stopped practice immediately to run to her. I was furious because I did not understand what a bad environment I had created. My misdirected anger was toward the coach whom I felt was undermining my authority. That moment forever motivated me to create a stronger rapport with my players in the future. Nowadays I would probably allow the players do run to the coach no problem, but we might have to talk about a more mature way of greeting someone coming on a visit. It's also wise for a former coach to give a heads up to the current coach before showing up for a visit.

Now with my girl's teams we spend more time getting to know one another and developing an understanding. With boy's we start with a very high level of discipline and slowly ease up as the season progresses. Even so, both teams get time to get to know each other on court.

The genesis of the problem I had with the boy's team at this same school came at the very beginning. When I first met this team on the first day of practice, one of the players left a piece of paper on my car to insult my parking job. On the face of it, the wording and imagery on the note were inappropriate from a player to a coach. But, tt was meant to be a   joke. In the context of my own fragile state of mind, I did not take the joke. I was a young man who was going to be respected, and jokes like this with someone you don't know were not appropriate. After much wasted time and effort getting to the bottom of who did it, and then talking it out, I had already damaged some trust with the team. It is a very fragile time when you first get started with a team, and it's best to exhibit great patience, understanding, and sense of humor as you place your program into effect. The message here is to be very patient with teenagers. Even now, it's very normal for me to go to a school and have the kids hate me the beginning while I am busy loving them. By the end of the season they love me (at least most do), because they saw how much fun we began to have after the work was done. To this end, it was seeing Wayne Bryan in 1995 at a conference that changed my coaching forever. If you don't know Wayne, he is the father of the Bryan Brothers, a great coach himself, and an ambassador for tennis. He brings the fun. Seeing Wayne influenced me to the point of where I was sure in my next job interview for a high school coaching position I was sure to express, "This is going to be fun."

If you are a young coach, you need to first learn to set a tone of getting work done, and try to avoid being too friendly with players. Once players see you more as a friend than a coach, then that familiarity will make following directions more difficult. Even so, develop a strong mutually respectful tone on your team, and never lose your sense of humor.

CHAPTER THIRTY-SIX
Developing Doubles Teams

High school tennis lineups are formed differently throughout the country, yet having strong doubles teams is crucial to success. I offer a combined art and science to forming teams: Everyone on my teams play doubles, even in only in practice to work on specific skills, or help sharpen their teammates.

Doubles helps a player's singles play for various reasons. As mentioned in another chapter, for the most part I like my lineup to stay static throughout the regular season. However, having all players ready for a possible line-up switch due to team match-up, injury, or illness is very important. It's a very poor idea to suddenly switch a singles player into a doubles position if they have had very limited court time with that partner. For that reason, I like to have all my top players ready to go. There have been a few times that using a legal lineup switch of taking a singles player out of singles to bolster the doubles lineup worked well for two reasons: 1. We had enough depth in singles to not experience a huge drop off, and 2. The player was very well familiar with the partner she would play with at the #1 doubles position. When playing our main league rival which seemed to be a very strong doubles playing team, inserting her there helped us to sweep the doubles. Before you think about getting all tricky, realize that of the over 10 times I considered making such a switch, only 2 times did I carry it out. The other 8 times I wanted to make sure that one player could win one match, rather than having two players win one match. Some teams go to the extreme of taking two singles players out of singles to play doubles, so if they were to lose one or both of those singles matches, then you better hope that you win that doubles line, and the positions below to make up for singles losses.

So, now on to developing chemistry with your doubles teams. Here are some quick tips:

1. Start on day one to build doubles chemistry. While you are holding tryouts for those to make the squad, keep your top players busy with doubles, which also serves to condense their court space leaving more room for tryouts.

2. Give players opportunities to practice with multiple partners two or three different partners is enough. A round robin of A/B v. C/D, A/C v. B/D and A/D v. B/C not only helps players become familiar with their partner, but also to see how they look to the opposition.

3. Use a flighted play formula to sort players out I will explain this more below.

4. Look for teams that have great chemistry, even if it goes against conventional wisdom of team formation. If fact, some of the most effective doubles teams may do things that no one else does, which can make them very tough to play against.

5. Look for individuals who make the other players around them better. Good doubles   players, make good doubles teams. A good doubles team with great chemistry and blending of styles can be great. If you pair one great doubles player with one who might not know what they are doing, the better doubles player can assume more responsibility and you can simplify strategy for the one who is the lesser player.

6. Work on court positioning and poaching in the first week. Getting players to become aggressive in the center of the court can take

some doing, so it's best to start early. As soon as some status quo is established with how to play the net, it can be hard to break.

7. Play games that encourage poaching. In the games and drills section of the book there are some that work. Poaching drills can be very simple. Put a player at the net, make a feed from the same position a returner would be returning, have the net player move to the ball and hit it between the two players. Simple. Many reps of poaching can be a great start. I am reminded of the time my team played against a great time, but my players were commanding the center of the court. Grand Slam doubles champion Vic Seixas was present, and could be overheard praising my players for dominating the middle of the court.

When I get my top players on one court playing doubles I may have six players to each court. Having them play tie-breakers with winner stays on can work to keep them busy. Sometimes regular tiebreakers can go too long, so you can substitute the 9-point tie-breaker, which goes to 5 points, and you win by one point only. They are exciting, and a great tool for starting tiebreakers well. Using the 9 point tiebreaker you may be able to get 8 players on the court if they rotate in quick succession. Tip: Give a special prize to teams that can win three straight tiebreakers.

When conducting tryouts, and then to select and order my doubles teams, I developed a flighted play metric that I like. Take four players: A and B vs. C and D, A and C vs. B and D, and so on. Have them play tie-breakers, and write down the score of each. On the adjacent court, E, F, G, and H can do the same thing. If there is a long TB that goes beyond 7-5, I like to note it as 7-6, because it was close, but I don't want players to gain an advantage simply because they won a longer Tiebreaker.

Let's say A scores 28, B scores 26, C scores 22, and D scores 24, then C would move down into the next lower group, and the top finisher from the next group down would join A,B and D to form a new round robin group. From the first group, the lowest scoring person moves down into the second group, the highest scoring person from a group moves up to the higher group. If you see a very dominant pair of players, you may move both of them up, and move two players down. (You are the coach!).

The benefits of this way of playing is that each point counts, and you can more accurately quantify if someone is a good doubles player. Conversely, simply tracking set scores can be misleading, as a 6-1 set may have had numerous deuce games, while even in a 6-4 set, one player may have not had much of any chance of breaking the opponent's serve. Another benefit is that it has a relatively predictable amount of time that it takes to complete a set of tiebreakers, and by using 9 point Tiebreakers, Set, or Match Tiebreakers you can vary the amount of time dedicate to the rotation. If you put some players out to play sets on two courts then one set could be quite fast, done in 20 minutes, while the other one could take an hour and 15 minutes to complete, which throws your practice into upheaval.

Over the course of a few days, the cream rises to the top. I repeat this process for two to three days, and then it becomes quite obvious who my top team, and maybe my top two teams are for the season. This is a great way to prepare for a time when a lineup switch may be necessary, and also prepare for post-season tournaments where singles players now become doubles players. You can begin to see if someone can play easily with anyone, or if two players have little or no chemistry on the court.

Once you have decided that a particular pairing should become a set team, you can remove them from the grouping, or keep them in the same group at all times, using them as a test team to try the other teams against. If you removing the set top teams, the remaining players continue in this process until it's obvious that more teams have been formed. After I have formed four to six doubles teams formed, a more formal challenge system of playing sets takes place. Ultimately, playing and winning sets as a team is more important than playing the tie-breaker system. Besides, I doubt that players would accept the round robin rotation as a way to make a final decision.

Once those teams are formed, take a closer look at each team. Are they playing on the ideal return sides? Do they know which player holds serve more easily? Have them experiment with using signals for poaching, or how and how much they talk between points. Each team has one weakness in they way they cover the court or holes in their game, so look for those and correct them or show the one player how to cover for the other's relative weakness.

Here are some considerations to decide if a team will complement one another:

1. Is there a fast player paired with a slower player? Of course two fast players is nice too, but it might not be a great idea to have two slower players, in order to have one who can get back to cover a lob.

2. Do you have a power player paired with a control or spin player? The variance in styles of hitting can really throw another team off, when the ball comes off your team's racquets in a dramatically different fashion.

3. Two tall players paired can be quite intimidating to another smaller team especially if they volley well and have solid overheads. The smaller team may feel like there is nowhere to hit. When playing against taller players in doubles, its a great idea to keep the ball low to the net.

4. Righty and lefty with forehands on the outside (high school players don't often serve to the T) Of course if playing a team that serves to the T, switch this. There are many opinions on how to pair righty's and lefty's, but keep in mind when their forehands are on the outside, they can be lobbed down the middle, and when their forehands are on the inside they can be lobbed to either corner with great effect.

So think through and experiment with forming your teams. Start with science, but move on to art and allow your players to become doubles artists.

CHAPTER THIRTY-SEVEN
No-Cut Teams, Boy's and Girls

When you are running a high school team, an ideal ratio of players is 4 players for every court. When you have that ratio players can easily play singles or doubles in any given practice. Sometimes I have had more than a 4:1 ratio and it means a little bit of shuffling players around. Some teams are extremely large. When you have a 6:1 ratio or greater, then it's time to have some courts with 6 or more players playing at the same time.

Here are some creative ways to use court time and have players productive even when not on court:

1. Create stations where a certain task occurs on one court, another task on another court, then an off court conditioning or mental game task. Rotate players by a 10,15,20 minute schedule.

2. Warming up: 6 players can rally on one court with pairs of players playing down the center of the court, and 2 sets of 2 players rallying in each alley.

3. Do you have way too many players? 3 players can be on one side, 6 players on the other, and players can sub in from one rally to the next. Every couple of minutes players can rotate to the other side so every gets a chance to be the lone player on their side. Or you can use a certain

amount of shots that a player hits before they rotate out, or balls that come their way.

4. Buy some portable nets, rope, or caution tape to give players a 'net' to rally over in an extra space. Players need to be mindful of balls flying in different directions.

5. If you have a hitting wall use it. Give players assignments to hit a certain number of shots, hit a target on the wall so many times, or ask them to come up with some creative ideas.

Singles: Team Singles is a great game that can be played with 4-10 players on each side. You can motivate the players by eliminating them by number of errors made. Players line up taking turns hitting shots in the same point. So when player 1, hits the first shot, then player 2 must hit the next shot followed by 3 and so on... This game is a great drill to help players to learn to recognize what the effect of their shot is. It's amazing how much more clearly players who are standing still can see where the player in front of them has hit and can anticipate much better the possibilities of where the opponent might hit the ball.

CHAPTER THIRTY-EIGHT
Diet, Drugs and Alcohol

There is some irony in working with gifted athletes, especially those who train very hard. They can gain a sense of their own invincibility very easily. Some come to believe that they are so talented or so well trained that their body can handle eating junk food with empty calories. A smaller percentage believe that they can participate in recreational drug use with little or no side effects. I have suspected players of being drug or alcohol abusers, and I have known that some were using. In each case I did something to make sure that the player knew I cared about their overall health.

To handle the diet aspect, I ask my players to write down everything they eat for 3 days, and include the size of the plate in which the food was served. That alone can be enough of a shock to the system of the player, when they realize exactly how many soft drinks they consume, or how many empty carbohydrates, etc. From there, we can talk about making some changes like maybe only having one soda per day, and to dramatically increase the amount of water that they consume. We can talk about increasing slightly the amount of vegetable matter, and great sources of high quality protein to replace the protein that was scraped for the last remaining fragment.

Recently, I was shocked by an article that showed case study research in regard to the high levels of recreational drug use among athletes. Surprisingly, Basketball players score quite low in drug use, while Lacrosse players scored the highest. What was alarming was that Tennis players scored more closely with Lacrosse players. It's worth having a discussion with your players. It's important not to come across as cop or school mom.

One player I knew was using marijuana and it was not really much of a secret, since his parents knew, and it seemed like it might have even been condoned in the household. Even so, I had a discussion with the player in regard to his use, and while he did not stop using, and there seemed not to be anyone at the school who wanted to follow up, I did my piece. It all came apart however when the player skipped a team trip to a tournament to go with his friends and cut school instead. Our team did poorly without him, and he was then suspended from the team. I have no way of knowing if I had any impact on the young man's life, but it was worth a try.

Another player would come to practice and seemingly would be under the influence of alcohol, but not enough so as to be obvious to everyone. I think I was the only one around who noticed. I spoke to the player and discussed with him a story about basketball coach Don Nelson and Chris Mullin, now a member of the Basketball Hall of Fame. Nelson bet Chris that he could not go a few days without a drink. When Mullin lost the bet, it made him come to grips with his addiction, and he then headed to rehab. From then on the player in question never came to practice looking as though they had imbibed in the last 24 hours. In recent years I have seen him as an adult and he now, like Chris Mullin is a very fit person. I assume that he got his drinking under control to pursue a more healthy lifestyle.

In conclusion, you should assume that there are players on your team that are doing drugs or alcohol, or eating very poorly. Look for the signs, express concern, and have the discussion. When the player is out of control in these areas, it will certainly hurt them, and many times will hurt the team.

CHAPTER THIRTY-NINE
Training / Education

Soon USATennisCoach will be offering a high school tennis coaching certification. This book will be one of the main texts for the initial exam. USATennisCoach will offer three levels and a collaborative approach to helping you take your coaching career and teams to the next level.

Obviously there are many other training opportunities in your area. The PTR offers a Certification for those working with 11 to 17 year olds. The USTA offers High School Coaches clinics. In NorCal the USTA partners with the USPTA to have a high school coaches workshop on one full day of our Division Convention, which is normally held at Stanford University.

The Positives:

* You can hear from great coaches on a topic that might be just what you need.
* You can network with other coaches from around your region and make a friend, and possibly fill out   your schedule.
* It can be a spring board to become a certified Tennis Professional, if you aren't already one.
* You can network with tennis professionals who may assist you with your team.

The Negatives:

* Some presentations are given by those who may have never coached high school tennis.
* Often the emphasis is on elite player development, so it might not help your beginners.
* There is not a systematic approach.

I have attended many professional tennis conferences, trainings and workshops, and found that I had   to put it all together myself, then make it my own.

Part of what has motivated the writing books and the creation of a high school tennis coaching certification is to provide you with a much more systematic approach to looking at your season.   This book is designed to be an A to Z on high school tennis.

I am especially conscious of the difficulties in translating college tennis to high school tennis.   College coaches recruit their players.   The players all have different schedules. The college team represents a very low ratio of player to coach.   The players for the most part are very motivated by excellence in tennis.   None of the players are there just because their friends are doing it. The hours they can put in on the court with fewer players per court are much more.   College coaches also work with players whose games are very well developed to a 5.5 to Open Level. Some high school leagues don't have a player who plays at a 5.0 level. Most likely the average high school varsity player is a 3.0 to 3.5 player, maybe lower.

When you go to the conferences be sure to arm yourself with great questions like "What would you do with beginners who come to the team and in two weeks time they need to be ready to play a match?"

Ultimately, go do it, I strongly urge you to get out into the greater tennis community and gain as much knowledge as you can.

CHAPTER FORTY
Beginner to Player

...in two weeks!

Week One

Day 1: Ball Possession Skills Have Players Toss balls back and forth underhand. Do "Downs, Ups, and Flip Flops". Have players rally to themselves. Then have players choke up on the racquet to the top of the grip and have miniature rallies over the net. They then can join in with other players and struggle or sit. Sometimes brand new players can be given the option to sit out of drills or games until they are comfortable to join in with the others.

Day 2: Rally Skills Have players toss balls back and forth over the net underhand, bouncing the ball to their partner. Do Downs, Ups and Flip Flops. Have players Rally in the Service Boxes over the net trying for a 10 shot rally. Players participate in every other activity.

Day 3: Rally and Tap Serve Repeat the activities of Days 1 and 2. Make your own mix of activities. Add a 'tap in' serve. Have players practice with racquet up by their shoulder and simply tap the ball up and over the net. Players can strive to make 5 out of 10.

Day 4: Volley Like a Wall Repeat Days 1 and 2. Introduce the volley, but having the players act like a wall, and simply let the ball bounce off their strings and over the net.

Day 5: Serve, Play and Return Have players practice making a serve, then hitting a shot. Introduce the Return of Serve with a simple turn and bunt motion.

Week Two

Day 6: Two New Players, Two Experienced - Doubles Go through a complete warm up. Pair a brand new player with a somewhat experienced player against another new player and a somewhat experienced player to learn to play doubles. If a new player double faults twice in a game, the somewhat experienced player can 'Pinch Serve' for their partner. Play a set, experienced players explain scoring as they go along.

Day 7: Three New Players, One Experienced - Doubles Go through a complete warm up. Have one experience player play with three brand new players in set of doubles. No 'pinch serve'. Have players report back on what they feel they need to do better to play. What are the confused about in regard to positioning, scoring, or other matters?

Day 8: One New, One Experienced - Tiebreaker Go through a complete warm up, and briefly explain how to play a tiebreaker. Have an experienced player play a tiebreaker of singles with a new player.

Day 9: Two New Players - Supervised Set Go through a complete warm up, have new players play singles against one another with an experienced player supervising and correcting any starting position errors.

Day 10: Four New Players - Supervised Doubles Go through a complete warm up. Have new players play a set of doubles, with an experience player supervising.

CHAPTER FORTY-ONE
Large Group Games - Triple Threat

The final 15 to 20 minutes of practice I love to play large group games. Each of my large group games forms a triple threat. 1. They each have an element of nearly continuous action, so players are almost always in motion we play fast enough that it becomes a blend of aerobic and anaerobic workout. 2. I will briefly stop a game to praise great execution or help make minor adjustments, so players learn on the fly with everyone watching. Players seem to have a high tolerance to stopping the game for about 30 seconds while they all learn something from what they just witnessed. 3. There are singles and doubles elements to each game. More important than the triple threat is that it's fun. Players barely acknowledge that it was a workout, and I don't talk about it. Also, they don't realize how much they have learned until they go to play and can see big leaps in performance.

Monkey in the Middle is a group game is for advanced beginners through advanced junior players, and can be included in a cardio workout. Players will get maintain a good pulse rate, learn to move well forward and diagonally, make quick decisions, become very aggressive at net, and be well-prepared for any sort of chaos on a doubles court.

Standard Version of the Game. Three champion players stand in a triangle shape with one player in the service boxes. When they enter the service boxes, the player who is the Monkey must not leave unless asked to rotate. The two supporting players must stay outside the service boxes, but may run alongside in the doubles alleys. If any of these players violate this rule, the other team gains a point. After each successful point won, they most rotate one position clockwise. After each point they lose, they must stay in their current position.

Challenging teams line up in three lines across the opposite baseline. Two lines are at the singles sideline, and the third is at the center line. The player in front of the center line plays with the players at the front of the other two lines as a team. They win or lose as a team.

The center position is also known at the Monkey Line. The ball is fed to the player in the Monkey Line, who takes the shot and transitions forward into the service boxes. They may hit one shot on their way into the service box. The Monkey must not leave the service boxes, and the support players must not enter.

The challenging team must win three straight points to become the champion team. However if one point is lost, then all three players first evacuate the court safely to allow for play to continue, then they go into the next line in order from the one in which they started. It's best to begin the game fairly slowly, directing traffic, until everyone in the group knows exactly what to do.

The First Feed: Give a ball easy to handle and transition. The Monkey moves forward to hit a forehand approach, and continues to the net. They must be inside the service boxes prior to their second shot. If the challenging team wins the point, the champion team stays put, and the second feed is made.

The second feed goes to the Monkey's forehand volley. If they win the point, the third feed may go to the forehand or backhand volley depending on the player. As coach you know who needs encouragement and who needs to work on their backhand volley.

Eventually, everyone in the team or group must be able to make a great backhand volley to win the game. It's amazing how patient players are during the game. If you stop and model good volley technique for 5 seconds, quite a bit of coaching can happen during the game. Do not talk for more than 30 seconds in the middle of a game.

Safety. Balls must not be struck from the back forward unexpectedly. The losing champion team must get out of the way of the winning champion team. Courts with little room to easily pass by nets require that all players pass the net before the next feed.

Variations for higher level players. The first ball must be taken out of the air. Overhead on first shot and towards the end of the game to challenge the champions. Unpredictable feeds, slice, top high low.

Variation for lower level players. All shots must land in the service boxes, support players play a few feet behind service line. Feed goes to champion team since a high percentage of first feed shots are missed by lower level players. All feeds go to forehand.

Send me an email to bill@pattonschooloftennis.com, for a free .pdf of large group games.

CHAPTER FORTY-TWO
Managing Cheating

When I was a kid, I may have watched too many episodes of Superman where he defended Truth, Justice, and the American Way. Now, although I am much more sophisticated in my understanding, I still carry some idealistic notions such as that one. In our game, it's important for every fair player to stand up against every cheater to help them make the switch. It's for their own good.

Since the original publication of this book, I have now also written:

How to End Cheating in Junior Tennis: 21 Ways to Eat an Elephant

That book has drawn praise from Bill Mountford of the USTA, and also numerous 5 star reviews from influential coaches in the United States and abroad. I highly recommend that you get one and it can be found for only $0.99 on Amazon.

Cheating is a habit, and for those who have cultivated that habit, most likely they do it, because it aided them in winning more matches, and more easily. The primary problem is the short sighted view of the value of winning over character development. The good news is that cheating can be unlearned. The question is: How or why did the cheater develop this habit. Probably the player made a bad call once, and no one seemed to notice and if they did, they did not say anything. Then the made another bad call, and they won a game. Then they made two or three calls in a match and won the match.

Do these players think the following thoughts? 'A few bad calls help me win more.' 'I'm not good enough to win without it.' 'If I lose my parents will yell at me.' 'I want to make my coach proud, and I see all the players in our group doing this.' 'If you are not cheating you are not trying hard enough.' We know that these are some of the thoughts that can be running through the minds of players as they play. Many times they are sub-conscious thoughts, so getting the root of them may not be all that easy to do. The onus is on coaches and parents to teach character development above results.

The problem, of course, is that when there is a large audience and the bright lights are on, this player will not be able to perform their magic. They won't be able to take a point or two, by winning now, they cripple themselves by developing a habit of taking the easy way out. Help these players early in life for the health of their game, and the health of the overall sport of tennis.

Now, let's talk about what cheating is not. It's not making one mistake in a match. Making calls is a difficult task. It's fairly difficult in a match with many close balls to be 100% accurate when you are moving. It's even more difficult when the ball is traveling over 80 mph. Look at the situation: the ball can be going one way fast, and the player going the other way. If a player makes two bad calls, that does not make them a cheater because they could have a vision problem. Three bad calls and whether they are a cheater or not does not matter. You both need help in this match. The player needs help with their calls, and you need protection against them.

From many years of coaching, and running USTA tournaments at the open and lower levels (although it could be different at higher levels), I see that approximately 80% of bad calls are a simple mistake. You might make a bad call someday. About 15% of bad calls are made because the person actually saw it out, but that may be because they want to win so bad, that they are psychologically blinded, or they just don't see well. About 5% of bad calls are because it's break point, and 'if I call this ball out I win the game or the set', the player has made up their mind that balls barely touching the line are out, and balls on the line will be called out if they really need the point. This spring I saw a player make a bad call against my player on a set point. The ball was clearly on the line, and the player clearly intended to steal the set. When he looked up at me immediately after making that call, his face contorted into one of "you caught me".

You can recognize the attitude of the player, and treat them accordingly. Immediately after a very close call, study the behavior of your opponent. Do they avoid eye contact with spectators and/or the opponent? Do they seem to be testing you to see if you will confront them? Do they break into a sinister smile? Another instance against a very wealthy school, I noticed the player made a bad call, caught the ball, then nodded to onlookers as though to acknowledge "Yeah, I'm a bad boy". It was so cute. Do they look around to see if anyone saw what they did? Any of these can be a sign that you are dealing with a deliberate cheater.

On the other hand, its best not to jump to conclusions. Don't be too tough on the kid who thinks he made the right call.

Those that are the criminal cheaters, whether coaches or players, are hoping for more for their efforts. They must subconsciously at least, know the effects that their cheating has on opponents:

1. The element of surprise is on their side. The shock value of the cheating may also affect the opponent for a few more points.

2. If their opponent is upset about the call, the negative emotions the opponent feels can disrupt their mental game.

3. The opponent may react to losing out on some close calls by attempting to play the ball much more safely to avoid bad calls. This would give the cheater a decided advantage.

It's important to get a lines person after a pattern of three calls has been established to make sure the outcome of the match is not decided completely by bad calls.

Coaches Who Cheat

Some coaches have their own private code of conduct which allows them to use illegal lineups. Some of these same coaches can be very sophisticated in the way they rationalize this to themselves and the team. In college play the rules and/or enforcement of 'stacking' the lineup are fairly liberal. So a high school coach may fantasize about being a college coach and 'prepare the kids for college'. Or they may have a belief that upper class men are always better and more mentally strong than younger players, so that allows them to keep a much better player who is a sophomore or freshman lower on the ladder, and not even allow them to challenge for the proper spot. I have known one coach whose modus operandi seemed to be to study the depth of teams league wide, and if say every team seemed to have two good players, then he would flip-flop his #2 and #3 players to assure at least one victory from the two spots. I saw this same coach do this at various positions over the period of a few years, which allowed me to discover his pattern.

When a coach stacks their lineup, it can succeed in making the opposing players upset for the same reasons above. Stacking allows that coach to know which match ups are in play, but creates an element of surprise to the opposing coach. This can force the other team to change their game plan on the fly. What do you do? In preparation for matches with that coach I previously mentioned, I began to tell my team, "It's not a matter of if they are going to cheat, it's just a matter of what it's going to be this time. Every match is a unique challenge, and this team is even more unique because of the element of surprise. Don't be surprised. Each player beat the player in front of you; that's all you can do."

Those people help you to be ready for anything. If as a coach you keep your cool, and are prepared to make a shift in game plan ahead of time, that can give your team a sort of moral compass. The coaches reaction to these problems with other teams can set the tone. You don't have to react emotionally if it's not a surprise, right? Instead, pity the poor team that has to look in the mirror with shame.

Why have self-doubt? We knew what was coming, and we were prepared and confident. Again, if you are expecting something at any time, then your mind is not distracted. If the players know that the game plan can change because of a change in the lineup, they become more emotionally flexible, which is part of a great mental game.

Over the years, I have noticed the interesting fact that teams do not play as well when their coach stacked the lineup. My personal belief is that they harm themselves when they carry the guilt of knowing they are cheating. When you feel like you don't deserve to win, will that help your confidence at the end of the match? Also, if they do win and the match can be disputed, then what is the point? It is tough to go through life and know that you cheated when you won the big match. You will always wonder if you could have won it without cheating. I hope these thoughts provide insight into why you can take it in stride.

I have disputed a few matches, and never gained the desired outcome in my protest. The only benefit gained was that I put those coaches on notice that we were not going to take it.

Perhaps the best solution is used in Southern California, where 3 singles players each play one set against each other. Then the three doubles teams play one set against each other. Also, I hear that when one team has secure 10 out of 18 possible wins then either team may begin substituting players into the line up. This is great on many levels, because there is the potential of three great sets of play, and the amount of play on the day is shortened provided each team has at least 6 courts on which to play the matches.

CHAPTER FORTY-THREE
How Players Manage Their Match

If a player is making bad calls or acts in a way meant to intimidate, distract, or bully, then it's important for the player to manage the situation. Almost always, cheating must be dealt with directly.

I have a rule of thumb for my players. The first call you disagree with, simply look at the player, get eye contact, then look at the place the ball landed. Sometimes the nice the opponent who sees this responds with, "Did you think that was good?" You then say, "Yes," as they can tell that you disagree, and after a moment of reflection, they realize that they were not 100% certain of their call. They then give you the point. I have seen this happen, and at that point you just made a friend because of a bad call. Give people a chance to be honest, and you will be pleasantly surprised.

Even if the opponent does not reverse their own call, in a very gentle non-verbal way, you or your player will have put them on notice that yes you are watching their calls. They may decide at that point to be more careful with their calls. When you gain eye contact with them, you can see their attitude. I get concerned immediately if the opponent does not allow eye contact after a bad call.

If there is a second bad call, call the player by name. "Hey Mike, are you sure about that call?" Adding the name takes away the power of anonymity. Some players cheat because they think you don't know them and you will never see them again. When they hear their name called, there is power there for you in the conversation. Of course, 99% of the time they will say they are sure about their call. If you think the ball was squarely on the line, you may ask the opponent to show you where it bounced. You can read a lot about their attitude as they show you how they saw it. See where they show you. Sometimes I see a player almost point to the line, then at the last moment they point to a place just barely out. When they point to a spot that is clearly not where it landed, I begin to think they can't see very well.

On the third bad call, get a lines person. If the player can't see or is psychologically blinded, then it's only fair for a lines person to make the match fair. If they are a criminal, then you have protected yourself from further crimes. In your mind, always assume that the opponent has some type of vision problem which is outside their control. It's a nicer feeling for you.

My friend Styrling Strother does something bold with his players. After bad calls, he has his player bring the other to the net for a chat. Styrling wants his players to directly confront the other player. "I see what you are doing, and you are going to respect me, and you are going to respect this sport. So no more bad calls; are you clear? If not, then I will be writing a note to the Athletic Director and your principal."

When it comes to bullying types of behavior, consider how you want to approach it in a way that works for you the player. I give my players three choices:

1.   Take charge of the match from getting the balls, to being first on court, to spinning the racket first, and asserting yourself. A battle may ensue. Win it.

2.   Be passive all the way through. Make the opponent do everything, including changing the scoreboard. Of course, watch them. Let them use up their energy being in control. Save yours and don't feel bad about it. However, make a stand on issues of calls, and

calling the score correctly.

3. Some players put a towel in a place where they know you can see it. Ask them to remove it. They must. Read the rulebook, *Friend at Court* so that you know all the things that are not allowed. It will empower you to know the rules of tennis.

The question you have to ask yourself is, *Can I tolerate it without distraction?* For instance if the opponent is giving you looks that are meant to intimidate, can you look away? I teach my players to simply not look at the annoying behavior that a player might have so it's not in their mind.

Some problems can only be helped by your coach. "Coach, can you please ask the other coach to tell them to stop doing ____?". Sometimes we meet coaches who yell instructions across the courts while people are in the middle of a point right in front of them.

Outright attempts at physical intimidation must be dealt with immediately. At a high school invitational tournament, one of my players was crouching to pick up a ball stuck in the fence. The opponent, seeing that she was in a vulnerable position, hit the other ball fairly hard and it seemed she was aiming at her head. It missed by two feet, and I saw the look of intention on the girls face. In short, the problem was confronted, and the other coach took care of business with his player. There were definitely moments of conflict on this issue, and I was willing to create some conflict for the safety of my player, and for those who would play this girl again in the future. Any kind of threat of physicality must be addressed.

CHAPTER FORTY-FOUR
Arrogance and The Rules - A Story

Just yesterday my 10th place team faced the first place team. They did not bring any more than the minimum of 10 required for varsity play. They have enough to give our players a match, but they chose not to bring them. They arrived less than 10 minutes before the match. I guess they felt like they might not need to warm up against us. Even so, with them arriving in such a short time prior to the match I offered to allow them to do introductions of players immediately so that they would be allowed a 10 minute warm up with the opponent. The coach accepted and the players appeared non-plussed by the arrangement. The match proceeded.

After the first game the opposing team's assistant coach coached his player, even though our league rules state that you must wait until the third game of the set to coach. I questioned him about this, and he stated that he was within the rules. I responded that he was not. Within a few minutes I got an answer from the commissioner of the league for all sports that essentially sided with me. I expressed that to the coach. He grumbled in acknowledgement.

Later, the head coach came along and in a very disrespectful tone condescended to me with "The collegiate coaching rule has been in effect for two years". I asked him, "So you are saying the commissioner got it wrong?" He affirmed, "Yes the commissioner got it wrong." All of this took place in the center of activity of the match with parent's listening in on the conversation.

Shortly thereafter, the parents complained that finding our courts was not easy, although I had given very explicit instructions for getting to our courts. If they had read them, they would not have complained. The assistant coach then griped that I had forced the girls onto the court with no warm up. I knew it was time for me to walk away as I began to feel a bit angry, and did not want to respond to what was being said. I called my AD to apprise him of the ongoing situation, and we formed the following strategy:

I have now written a letter that was approved by my Athletic Director that is being sent to the other coach's Athletic Director and the Commissioner of the league. I have asked for a written apology from the other coach, also signed by an administrator for creating confusion about the rules, and for the embarrassing behavior directed at me. 95% of the time at least you will be in very pleasant or at least civil interactions with opposing coaches, friendships are formed. Sometimes you have to be the bigger person, keep your cool, while bringing to light the problems that exist. I am quite certain that these coaches have been bullying teams into believing that the rules are something other than what they are. Taking the longer view to see if something is worth fighting, for the good of everyone in the league is something to consider.

At the end of the season meeting, I watched with great interest and studied the face of the opposing head coach as the comissioner explained that he was wrong. That explanation did not stop the coach from arguing with the commissioner in front of all the coaches. That was enough for me.

CHAPTER FORTY-FIVE
Amazing Kids

Last year an amazing kid decided that he would bring back the high school tennis program at his school. The school had not had a boy's tennis team for at least one year, and he wanted to play. So this freshman boy, recruited his friends in 9th grade and they got a squad going with over 12 players. He recruited his dad to be the coach. So, coaches empower students and support them when they want to do something that will have a lasting positive impact on the sport at their school.

This year, another school started the work of bringing back tennis, so rather than play in the league, they asked teams in our league if they could play on the bye. We arranged these matches as exhibitions. The coaches agreed that the match would be a forfeit, allowing the better team to play its lower level players to give the new team some competition that would be realistic. It was a fantastic success. Next year that team will join our league as a full fledged member. They wanted to play us twice, but we had to keep our own goals in mind, so we only played them once.

Raymond was 5'2 and 85# when he joined the tennis team. He was so small, I sent him to court 8, as far away as he could be from court 1 where the top players were. It was the first day of tryouts and I was working with a team I had not coached before. My friend offered to help me sort the players out some. Shortly after the beginning of our session, Mitch approached me with great urgency and chirped "You better watch this kid on court 8". About 10 seconds after seeing Raymond use his entire 85 pounds to hit every ball, I asked him to come to court 1, where he began to rally with the top 3 returning players. It was quite obvious that he would be vying for the top spot on the team. Within a day or two Raymond played the #1 from the year before winning 6-1, clearly becoming #1. For a team that had rarely been higher than .500 and in great years could finish second in league, or if due to heavy graduation could fall to the second division in league, Raymond became the lynchpin to changing the culture of tennis at the school. We finished 10-4, 14-0, 11-5, 14-2 during his time there, winning the championship in his second year. He was a 4 time finalist in league championship singles and doubles combined winning a singles title and a doubles title.

CHAPTER FORTY-SIX
The Ball Does Not Bounce Funny

Tennis is not a funny game. It's very rare that any kind of luck can impact a match in a significant way. Many sports have a much greater element of luck, or facets of the game you can't control. In tennis, the ball rarely if every bounces funny, one dramatic play cannot radically alter the score, one player can't play incredibly well and lift the entire team, etc. There isn't an official to give a catastrophic bad call to your team.

Upsets and/or bad losses are pretty rare. The better team wins. So on the day learning to channel all your efforts to playing as close to your best performance gives you the best chance at an upset. My experience tells me that if the heavy favorite team does not put in a full effort, and also come ready to compete all the way until the end of the match, then the door is open. Teams ripe to upset another must first focus on effort level one point to the next, believing they can win, but also hoping and trying to cause the other team to not play as well. As a favorite, creating a baseline of effort and respect for the opponent is paramount to avoiding the trap of an upset.

Now, what to do after your team has lost to a team to which they ought not to lose? It seems that each time I have taken over a team for the first time, in that first season we have an episode of one very poor performance. Whether due to a lack of respect for the other team, a simple unwillingness to put forth a full effort, or any other reason, I don't think a coach can fully protect his team from something like this happening one time. Great coaches use that experience to teach players about respect and giving best efforts every time on court. Just a week ago a team I am coaching was facing a team I thought we could rout, if we gave our best effort. I believe my players interpreted what I was saying incorrectly. The way they played it seemed they got the message that we did not have to give a full effort to win. They reverted back to the same type of competitive level that they have used in the past, and our team became victims of the upset.

During the match some players, on court were obviously relaxing and joking around, and giving less than 100% effort. The team as a whole did not have a spirit of competitiveness and determination to fight until the very end of the match. The players who were not on court were not engaged in the matches and seeking to pump up their teammates, they were more concerned about socializing and having snacks. Multiple times during the match I redirected them not to stand in a circle facing away from the competition, but to go support their teammates. After the loss, we had a meeting, where I expressed to them that they had failed to compete, failed to support, failed to give 100% effort, and failed to show themselves strong and wise. I asked captains to weigh in on the failure, and they did. We did succeed at learning from the experience.

So the next day at practice at every break, I shared a story of teams that learned the hard lesson, and how moving forward they gave full effort and determination. That is the opportunity to created a cultural shift in the program. Sadly, the players may need to feel the disappointment of losing or having a match that was way too close for comfort in order to fully grasp what the coach is telling them. "When the student is ready, the teacher appears", has been a great quote through the ages that captures this moment. It's the next moment that matters most.

With my winningest teams, I have sometimes felt sorry for the next team we play, if we lost in our previous match. As my teams have learned more and more how to compete, the sting of losing motivates them to the point where I know they are going to respond with a tremendous effort and focus in matches moving forward, especially the very next match. In conversations with other coaches when talking about that next match, I have received comments about how well my team played and how the coach felt like they "Got run over by a truck". I then I explain how motivated the kids are after having lost a match.

The next match for my team that had failed so miserably showed considerable growth in my players. We faced our rival who were heavy favorites, because they have a veteran team, and half our team started the year holding a tennis racquet for the first time. The girls made me very proud by fighting for every point and making the match very close to the point where it ended very close to the darkness of late October. We had a chance to win, even though some of our players were facing personal adversity on the day. So, then I let them know how proud I was of them for that match and we know used that as a springboard for how we can compete moving forward.

Big wins can be very difficult to recover from, as they are emotionally draining. The amount of coping that it takes to wrap your head around a huge upset, and the recovery of having used up almost all your mental, emotional and physical energy puts the team at risk in the next match. I am quite proud of the fact that my teams have pulled upsets at fairly significant rate, and its something for everyone to strive for with their players. Nothing matches the elation of doing something that people thought was not possible. An example of this is when in the postseason team tournament my #9 seeded team beat #8 in the playoffs fairly convincingly, to win the right to play the #1 seeds. Almost immediately, it seemed we were preparing for a death march. Instead we put our full focus on planning to play the best we can possibly play. I offered to the team "One, or some of you may play the best match of your life today, so if it's you, let it happen. If it's not you don't force it, just do the best you can do". With at least 3 out of our 10 players playing the match of their young lives, we pulled the upset. However, moving into the match in the semifinals against the #5 seeds, some of our young players could not quite summon the same level of play. They were thinking about it too much. Emotionally they were spent from having played at an intensity they had never experienced.

The same type of thing happened with my girls team who were effectively a #10 seed, and beat #7 in a close match, then beat the #2 seeds in a nail biter that came down to the final third set tiebreaker, and ended with the girls dog piling the winning team on the court. Two days later, our team was quite visibly emotionally spent from one very close win, and one very emotional upset. We did our best to rest the players, but there is only so much capacity the players bring. In both of the above semi-final loses, I tried to be patient, but I found myself urging the players on more and more trying to push their buttons to little or no effect. Even so, the experience of having pulled an upset, then losing served a greater purpose.

Both of the above teams gained much higher seedings in the following year, and were able to secure sectional championships, which in California is equivalent to a state championship in some states. Quite an achievement from those players who learned to manage the energy levels necessary to be champions.

Another interesting factor from the one season to the next was that the effort level from match to match was very even and very close to 100% effort every time on court`. Also, the players seemed to manage the schedule of their lives to a better degree so that they would have a more balanced lifestyle, thus assuring they would have enough energy to compete at the highest levels among 450 schools in our area. I hope you sense how proud I am of those players, and that I have a lesson to share with you. I found these experiences very fulfilling as a coach.

CHAPTER FORTY-SEVEN
Appropriate and Innappropriate Behavior

Coaches, this is very serious topic to cover. As you know, every year coaches across the country get in trouble for shameful behavior. I would hope that every coach intends to keep their behavior up to the highest standards of integrity. So this chapter is here to help provide some guidelines for success in that area. Some behaviors that coaches use with players are great and that relationship that can be built up over the period of 2, 3, 4 or maybe even more seasons can be one of the most influential in a young life. So consider first what impact you want to have on that young life. The choices you make can have a lifelong positive impact on a person, be inconsequential, or maybe highly destructive. I know that this type of information is available in more general coaching trainings, but I feel compelled to share these thoughts.

Since you have already developed your coaching philosophy, and it more than likely includes some aspects of player personal growth, let's get practical about how to stay away from trouble.

1. Be the adult at all times and not a friend to the players.
Many times coaches in their 20s are pressed into duty and may be right out of a credential program teaching at a school. Or, a former player at the school who has now been asked to coach the team. It will be immediately tempting to want to be friendly with the players. Avoid

being friendly. Keep your behavior solely focused on the outcomes with your students. Even veteran coaches who have been at a school for a period of time will develop great relationships with the players, but you must avoid being a friend to the players. Once a form of friendship type of bond is established, that can be the first step in a slippery slope of declining behavior. Not all teenagers will play upon a friendship to gain some type of influence, but some will. It's best to protect yourself against this small minority of players, because once you fail in this area, it seems there is no going back without major consequences to the program. Even discussion or debate about politics can be a problem area, and any talk of religion can invite scrutiny about you and your program. The exception would be when your school has some type of affiliation in political or religious groups that encourage such discussion.

Having said that, I do create a fun atmosphere with my players, but I stay on this side of the equation by only giving high fives, and not discussing any close personal matters with my players. We only talk about things that directly affect the outcome of their growth as players and people.

2. Avoid being alone in a room with a member of the team. Instead move to a public place and/or one where there are other people nearby.

3. Avoid being alone with a member of the opposite sex, without contacting the parent. This includes driving a student home in the rare instance that something has gone amiss with transportation.

Follow these simple guidelines, and you will likely avoid any hint of second guessing.

CHAPTER FORTY-EIGHT
Story Telling and Creating Legends

Story of Cupcake

Wayne Bryan saved my high school coaching career. Before Wayne, I was not fun enough. This story is dedicated to him, because without his inspiration and direction, I would not have known what to do or what to look for in my players. In my first coaching job, I admired the rapport that some coaches in our league seemed to have with their players. I had failed to create that same type of rapport.

I would never have been so determined to take my team to see professional tennis, or do other activities with my teams in the name of fun. It was at an event in 1995 that I first met Wayne, and he gave his customary inspiring talk, about all the things coaches and professionals can and should do to make it fun.

In 1996, I took my team to go see the SAP Open (then by another name), the now-defunct tournament that was held in San Jose, and in various locations prior to that year. By chance that year, the tournament started on President's Day, so our players were out of school for the day. We planned to go for the night session, but a tournament friend of mine heard about our plan, and she donated her company's unused daytime tickets for the event. What a bonanza! We now had a chance to see a full day and night of tennis, and 20 kids from our team went.

As we arrived and were about to walk in, I held everyone up for a quick meeting. These were good kids, so I did not want to burden them with too many rules. Besides, what could go wrong in a controlled indoor arena environment? "Gentlemen , as we go in here, I want you to know the rules.", I plainly stated, "Rule #1, if you want to go home with us tonight, meet in section 203 at 9:00 p.m. We will leave from there, so anyone who fails to do that had better call their parents. (Sometimes you have to scare teenagers.) Rule #2, if you get caught doing anything wrong, you don't know me. Now repeat the rules back to me."

A look of excitement came over everyone in the group as we entered the arena. Not only had they never seen the facility, which as barely a few years old, but none had ever seen professional tennis live before. The San Jose Arena is an excellent piece of architecture with gleaming glass, stainless steel, chrome, white tile, and very well-lit. It feels like a palace.

Some amazing things happened that day. For one, the players realized that watching tennis live was awesome. They also learned that some matches can be very boring. I think they gained some empathy for me, because I have to watch every match they play. Two players managed to sneak into the player's lounge and eat some of the ATP player's food. I was happy to find out about after the fact, but not something you want to condone as an adult. (Come on, folks, sixteen-year-olds are supposed to do this stuff!)

I was able to show some of the players how points are won or lost while we were there sitting and enjoying the tennis. I could also help them understand the the difference is between a forced error and unforced error. Of course, there was some arguing by the opinionated player on the team about what which kind of error was which. When you see live tennis one of the advantages is that you can focus only on one player for a short while and give them your full attention. You can't see that very often on TV. Also, TV does not capture the speed of the ball the way live viewing does. Just about every person I meed seeing live pro tennis loves seeing the speed of the ball and some truly great shots. So our day had been very full, but it was about to get better.

The day session ended.

As we were preparing for the night session with almost a two-hour break, one player asked me if he could go get something to eat in downtown San Jose. It was certainly not the nice part of downtown. I thought 'no', but then I said, "Okay, but you have to use the buddy system. Three of you have to go. Two of you could easily be corralled, but three makes it that much harder, so sure got get Pizza." The three left immediately including a team captain, one other upperclassmen, and our very tiny freshman-- off to get pizza. The outcome of their excursion is now legendary.

When they came back, something seemed wrong. Our little Freshman's face seemed pale, and he seemed petrified. The team captain said, "Oh yeah, Coach, the Freshman thought we were going to be killed. When we were in the pizza place waiting, a rough-looking crazy guy came in asking for a cupcake. He said, "Do you have cupcakes?" We weren't sure if he was talking to us, or to the pizza people. He then raised his voice, "I said, do you have cupcakes?" He then continued shouting "Give me a cupcake! I want a cupcake. Give me a f-----g cupcake!" The whole team thought this was quite funny, and then it became our rally cry for the year. "Give me a cupcake!"

We used the word "cupcake" all season, and having gained a considerable amount of team bonding, we had the moral strength to play great against the two teams that we had lost to the year before. In the previous season, we had finished third, we went 0-4 against the two teams above us in 1995. It was disappointing to lose to those teams, since I was very confident that we had enough talent to win. So as we went through our 1996 season, after the pro tennis cupcake experience, we found ourselves 3-0 against our top competition. All we needed to do was knock off the second place team one more time to clinch the title. We would have to face them on the road, and we knew that they are a ferociously competitive team. The heavy weight of 26 years since owning a league title was hanging over the team. But I didn't want them thinking about history, because that would create too much pressure. I wanted them to think about.... a cupcake.

I hate cupcakes, especially dry ones. I hate frosting, and cake makes me thirsty. But this was clearly not about me.

The weekend previous to the big match, I was at a children's birthday party, someone asked me if I wanted a cupcake, of course I said "Yes, give me a cupcake!". As I internally replayed the story of the rough looking guy at the Pizza parlor smiled on the inside and went immediately to my car placing the cupcake on the dashboard where it would stay for 5 days, until the Thursday of the match.

On Thursday, we arrived at the match, and in the pre-game talk, I produced the cupcake, stating with a sense of bestowing honor, "Gentlemen, normally we give a small reward for matches well played, but today there is a special prize. Whoever wins today's clinching match gets this cupcake". Instantly all eyes on the team were hungry for cupcake. No one knew how dry it was, because they were not allowed to inspect it closely.

One thing you have to know about this particular rival school that we played on that day, is that if they have lost to you once, they are going to dramatically ramp up their efforts, and they will take blood oaths to one another, such as, "I promise for the remainder of my high school career, I will never again lose to (insert team name here)." They will even go one notch higher for a home match against a team they lost to on the road.

Each school had a unique home field advantage of playing on bad courts that they knew really well and how to play in those conditions. The match was very close as we traded victories. At first, my team was a little upset because the first and second doubles teams had been switched from the time before. We had swept those matches in our first meeting, so the coach was stacking his lineup to try to get one victory. It worked, but not the way you would think.

My #1 team played terribly against what had been their #2 team in the first meeting, and now we are down 0-1. However my #2 team played out of their minds and with incredible grit, defeating their #1 team from the previous match. I think my team was angry and they let that anger fuel them to play well. I overheard a player from the rival team's #1 doubles team say to his coach, "I can't believe we lost to their #2 team." The coach responded, "Don't worry, we got the win we wanted." The opposing doubles teams then turned to see that I was right there and had heard what they said. I could see them gulp when they realized that I had heard them.

After splitting four of the five singles matches, there one was left to decide the outcome of the match. As we neared the conclusion the final match was going into a third set, between Carlos who was about 5' 2" and 120 pounds, playing against their guy who was 6' 1", 195 pounds, and a starter on their basketball team. Little Carlos had really only one reliable play, the drop-shot lob combination. Carlos won the first set using that combination. The opponent, G, won the second set as he was hitting a few more good overheads.

Carlos began to panic. "Now just mix in a little drop-shot/passing shot because he comes in and starts drifting back for the overhead right away. This will surprise him, and he will have to get closer to the net, and then you can lob him again."

The set progressed, and Carlos was doing as well as he could. The opponent served for the match at 5-4, but Carlos broke him, held serve, and broke him again for the match, as the opponent simply had run out of the ability to hit any strong overheads, and was unable to move quickly back to retrieve balls. Pandemonium ensued as we clinched our first title in 26 years. One great sportsman from their team came to me and said, "Coach, congratulations on the championship; you guy's really deserve it." I was proud of that young man.

I went to my car, got the cupcake, brought the team together, and said, "Carlos, here is your cupcake." He instantly ate it without inspecting it in any way. I'm not sure how he felt after that, I guess I should have told him...

Sadly, the young man that congratulated me, was much-loved at his school, died in a car accident a few years later, killed by a drunk driver.

Tears stream down my face as I write this. At that school, there is a plaque in his honor in the main office, and a day dedicated to his memory where people are especially kind to one another. So even in the midst of what is a story about a team overcoming the challenge of another team to win a title, those little acts of kindness, sportsmanship and honor are the true magical treasures.

CHAPTER FORTY-NINE
Maynard and The Lawnmower

Some players just don't fit the mold of a classic style. So, even though we as coaches may have a vision of what we think must be, we need to be flexible to understand that we need to adjust our thinking. When I stopped thinking I had all the answers and took the time to examine every player for what they brought to a match, asking them what they felt they needed to work on and discussing it with them, my coaching took a leap. On my radio show (find a link on my website at www. 720degreecoaching.org) I interview some of the greatest tennis coaches in the U.S. and around the world. I hear one thing again and again: Great coaches are great listeners and also great observers.

I owe a huge shift in my thinking to Maynard. Maynard had a backhand that was one of the worst-looking shots I have ever seen. Bad-looking strokes need to be fixed, right? Maybe those strokes do not need to be fixed. Maynard's backhand looked like he was trying to start an upside down lawn mower suspended over his left shoulder by pulling a cord from his shoulder down in an arc to his waist on the opposite side, while applying a vicious corkscrew chop on the ball. The ball would come off his racquet fairly high in the air flying at least 6 feet off the ground over the net, and probably more often closer to 10 feet above the ground, then taking a skewed curve over the net. When the ball landed it took a big jump to the left.

As many coaches would, I set about working to fix his backhand. Over the course of two weeks, I tried to get him to go low to high and develop a flat or topspin backhand. During that time he worked very hard with me on this, but his results in challenge matches were terrible, as you can imagine. The transition was very tough on Maynard's match confidence, and he really put quite a bit of effort into it. With the regular season two weeks away and almost no progress being made because of the depth of habit he had developed by hitting this same shot for years, it simply was not worth the anguish, especially because he was a senior. I told him he could learn to better utilize this shot he hits.

When I actually stopped to watch him play, I noticed a fun pattern emerging. Opponents quickly figured out that Maynard had a weird backhand, so they would hit, one, two, three shots to it. Early on, his opponent's would incorrectly assume that Maynard would make an error. However, with very few errors, Maynard continued to make that corkscrew backhand. Players quickly got tired of this because they had a hard time with it. The big jump the ball took to the left was very difficult for them to time, and players at Maynard's spot of the lineup were no well equipped to deal with it. So, they would hit to his forehand and-- BOOM!--Maynard was now in control of the rally with his very penetrating forehand.

Maynard then learned to change the spin on the ball applying more or less spin, so he could control how much the ball jumped to the left. Once he mastered that, he was able to draw more errors and weak shots from his opponents.

Maynard also had a very strong first serve, and a very strange second serve. But his confidence soared because he had a game plan, and he became a strong varsity singles player.

During the course of the season, hundreds of times Maynard's opponents would hit two or three shots to his backhand and receive back the crazy ball. After the opponent decided they really did not like the result of hitting to the backhand, they almost reflexively chose destruction by hitting to Maynard's forehand. It was fun to watch. I realized I could have errantly destroyed Maynard's game by breaking down a stroke at the wrong time, thus wrecking his confidence. His tough play for the team, included winning some important confidence-boosting matches for himself and the team which helped set the table for a championship the next year.

CHAPTER FIFTY
27 Years One Amy

Amy is a young lady who just blended in with the team. She was respectful of the established order. One day she seemed to be having a bad attitude. It was early in my time coaching a new team, and I wanted to nip any problems in the bud early if I could. I took Amy aside and asked "Are we ok? How are you doing?". She responded by saying she was having a hard day. So, what I thought was directed toward me, which really was slightly directed my way, was not really meant for me. That early moment was pivotal in the relationship I have with Amy today.

This young lady had started in the doubles lineup, but then when I offered players a chance to try out for singles, she was in that group. Initially she came out as the #4 player, and her strokes were fairly unorthodox, but not as bad as Maynard. Amy played what used to be called a 'Chop' style of play. Nearly every ball she hits comes of with slice. Sometimes she floats the ball back to the baseline, where it rests nicely with no pace, other times she gives the ball a cutting slice that stays low, and still other times she bends the ball to the left or right depending on backhand or forehand. She also has a shot that very few players possess, its a high forehand volley overhead, struck just above her shoulder that takes the opponent by surprise and it makes for a great down the line winner. Amy moved up to #3, then #2 based on her early wins. She was winning convincingly, while those above her were losing matches. Amy earned the right to have challenge matches. She also got to play some matches at #1 when our team's top player was absent.

As our last place team, which was top heavy with two strong players at the top headed into post season, I was very confident that our top player, or Amy had a chance to be league champion. When our top player was unable to play the league tournament, Amy ascended to the top spot on our ladder, and went into the tournament as the #3 seed, even though she had beaten the top seed before, the top seed had played more winning matches in the #1 position for her school.

Amy knew that she would have to beat the #2, and #1 seeds in the same day. She took the matches one at a time. When I asked her how determined she was to beat the #2 seed she said "100.1%", which was funny to me, because I think she had listened when I said I don't like the concept of 110%. After a shaky start, she got her game together, and after a tight first set, she won convincingly to get into the finals.

In the finals, she was facing the girl who was voted "Player of the Year", but had not played a very good match in the semi-final. Her backhand was suspect in that match. We thought Amy could really pick on that shot. Unfortunately for Amy, the opponent's backhand was much more solid and mistake free. On an early 3-all point (deuce) in a no-ad game, Amy hit a ball squarely on the line that was called out. She had been hesitant to call for a lines person in the past, but this time she did not hesitate. We know and like the other girl, and it was clear to myself and the other coach that both girls were caught up in this big moment and were not quite themselves. That was true, because Amy was super human. Her determination level was supreme. She managed to come back from the missed call, winning the first set in a tiebreaker, but then... Her parent's arrived. Amy's parents are among the sweetest and nicest people you would ever want to meet. And, of course, Amy feels extremely nervous playing with them watching. Quickly she found herself in an 0-3 hole, with the opponent now playing much more powerfully taking control of the points quickly and finishing. The match seemed to be slipping away when she lost the second set 6-2.

The third set began with 6 consecutive breaks of serve, Amy would break serve, then have her serve broken. Mainly it seemed because the opponent would ramp up her own determination, having lost her serve game. Through out that third set, there were at least 10 balls that when the opponent hit them very hard, I thought "Amy is not going to get that... oh she did!". Amy's laser focus came to bear, and the other player inexplicably broke under the pressure and what had been a 3-all set, became a 6-3 win for Amy. Her championship represents the first ever tennis title of any kind in school history since the place was built in 1955. Congratulations Amy.

What makes her so special? Amy improved, especially in the field of play. Together we worked out her best game and she used it to go 16-5 on the season for a last place team. I believe she is the most improved player I have ever coached in my 27 years.

CHAPTER FIFTY-ONE
Match Day - On Court Coaching

The most important thing to know about on-court coaching on changeovers is that there is not a lot of information a player can take in and immediately apply. Early in my career I made the mistake of giving too much information, messing up my player's head with too much information to process. Generally, helping a player to simplify a match is generally farm more helpful than making it more complicated for them. Over time, I also learned that the change in a match may not be immediate after the information is given. For certain players no amount of technical information is going to help, if the player does not feel the mental and emotional support from the coach.

Be patient. When you give input during a changeover, you may see a shift in how your player plays during the next two games, and they may struggle initially. I have seen players need four full games to shift the strategy and begin to execute properly. Whatever you put in motion with your player on a changeover, I would advise that you stick with that game plan for a few more games. It may be tempting to go on the next changeover to attempt another change if you don't see the execution you want. Here is where I recommend praising the efforts of the player to make the change. Heck that kid trusted you enough to do what you said, now help them understand what they can do to execute the play a little better each time.

Give that the number one mistake made in on-court coaching is giving too much input, a good guideline is to talk to your player no more than twice in one set. There are exceptions to this. In fact, recently as Amy was in the midst of a very tough three set final, and seemed to be emotionally on a rollercoaster, she and I got together on almost every change over. In that case, I simply would find different ways to remind her of the same things we had talked about and also came to reassure her. Not every player will need that in a final match, but this was such a new experience for Amy she seemed to be feeling a little overwhelmed.

One of my favorite examples of being patient with the game plan also happens to be one of my favorite matches of all time. Peter was playing a much superior athlete, his opponent was taller, stronger, faster and had much more powerful strokes. Peter could easily have given up. After he was down 5-0 in the first, we talked about changing the game plan somewhat. He then managed to win a game before losing the set 6-1. We talked about another adjustment and mainly that Peter should run down every ball, and keep the ball down the center of the court, to take away easy angles from his opponent, and eliminate the other player's speed advantage. We wanted to test to see how long the other player can continue to hit great shots. Though Peter was executing better he was still down 4-1 in the second set, although it represented only one break of serve. One the face of it, many teenagers would cave in, seeing that the opponent had won the first set convincingly, and was now only two games from winning the match. In the mind of a player, it can seem to be a mountain to climb. In reality, it may only take 10-15 minutes to turn it around. Just as we hoped, since Peter made things just a bit more difficult, the opponent began to miss more shots, and Peter also adjusted to the speed and location tendencies of his opponent. The superior athlete served for the match at 5-2, and 5-4, Peter broke him each time. When an opponent gets to 5 and is about to serve, I instruct my players to "Look at him, and walk around on the court as though to say, 'there is no way you can close out this match'.". The pressure of serving out the match was getting to the opponent. The match went into a second set tiebreaker which Peter somehow won, then it was just about over. We didn't know it at that moment, but Peter's opponent clearly felt robbed and as though he should have already won the match, went 'down the tubes' losing 6-0 in the third in a nearly complete melt down blasting balls harder than he could keep them in the court. Peter and I had a nice laugh later.

Generally it's wise to wait until 5 games have been played to allow players to get into the flow of a match. Any player can get off to a rocky start and left alone, many can sort it out themselves, it's great for a player's confidence when they can do that. Coaches sometimes don't realize that they hurt their players resilience when they offer too much help too early. Some players are naturally slow starters. The best thing to do, is talk about after the match, how to prepare better for stronger starts. It can be a good idea to break the guideline if they are down 3-0 quickly with two breaks of serve against them. Sometimes a quick word of encouragement to help them take care of their own serve game can help immensely. If your player is quickly down 5-0, then it's going to be important to make some kind of change right then, because you want to make a strong start to the second set if you lose the first. In high school its very possible to lose a first set 6-0 or 6-1 and come back to win. The good news is that not a lot of energy is expended in that first set, leaving a lot of time and energy for two more to be played.

Outside of the 5th game coaching guideline, there are some exceptions for when I would coach at the 3rd game, or even (if the rules allow) the 1st game:

* You notice a glaring weakness in the opponent during the warm-up and first game. Note: Some leagues abide by a no-coaching on the first changeover rule, so you may need to wait until the 3rd game.

* The game plan was misunderstood, or obviously not effective.

* The player really wants and needs the emotional support, and other matches can afford your attention to be spent more on one player.

How Much to Say

It has been said that the attention span of a teenager is about 10 seconds or 42 words per input. Be sure to limit the sum of your content to that which can be said inside of 10 seconds. I have said way too much to my players on changeovers, then those players begin to think too much about what I said, rather than going on to play the match. A best practice is to think through what you might say before you get to the fence, you are more likely to be very concise. Over time, you can develop code words rich with meaning. So I may say, "Weapon, Positioning, and Her Backhand". The player, because we have developed this level of communication, knows to use their weapon 'confidence', that I want her to get into the best possible position for her shot, and work to attack the other player's backhand. One of our program staples is that we say often "Confidence is my biggest weapon".

Shifting your player's focus onto the weakness of an opponent, can help them not to worry about their own. Players often build up their opponent in their minds making them an almost invincible foe. Asking a player how they win their points or a new subtle trend they see in the match, can assist them in making mindful to shifts in strategy while also noting that they can win points. Often I like to ask a player what they see happening in a match because they are the ones hitting the ball, not me. Many times there are multiple matches to watch, I rarely see anything approaching 100% of a match. When coaching, often I start with, "I haven't seen a lot of this match; what is happening in this one?" or "I think I see her doing this... and you could do that... what do you think?" Occasionally, the player says something that is genius, so then of course, that's the plan from then onward. Listening to your player empowers them to be more thoughtful about their match.

Another thing to think about is how much energy to bring to the situation. Mainly, I like to be very calm and calculating. At rare times maybe 3 or 4 times in a season, I will bring a lot of energy to changeover and really urge my players on to increase intensity, competitiveness and/or effort level. Some players will want eye contact, others feel lonely if the other coach is coaching their player and you don't coach them. Other players prefer to be left completely alone and not receive any coaching, so gaining that player's trust that you aren't going to mess up their mind is very important. Learn how each player prefers to receive the information and you will become much better on changeovers.

On last tip, a little gem I learned from Dick Gould, one of the greatest coaches in the history of the world. Sometimes you are at your wits end, or their is no new information to give, and the match is in the balance. Go to your player and say "I have nothing new to say, but lets both look at your opponent, you nod your head like I just said something awesome. Then walk away from the fence and throughout the match, like I just said the magical thing that will make it impossible for them to beat you." Almost always, the player walks away from that playing very well. In a close match, this coaching ploy has been the deciding factor in a match. There is deep magic in what I learned from Dick Gould here, but let's not overanalyze it.

CHAPTER FIFTY-TWO

Match Day - Pre and Post Match Rituals

Pre-Match Rituals

Teenagers naturally seem to gravitate toward chaos prior to matches. The combination of release from their hours at school, and the anxiety or lack of anxiety about a match, can have them wanting to do everything but the proper preparation. They will fritter away time, hold a conversation, and generally participate in chaos, this is fairly normal for them. Teaching players great match preparation not only occurs in the phases of training, but also on the day of the match. Rather than explain every reason for everything, I will give you my own pre-match ritual, then imagine how many problems are solved by these guidelines:

Players should:

1. Arrive more than **30 minutes prior to the match**, and be on court practicing at least 30 minutes left before start time. Many schools bus the players, so that makes it easy, but when players provide their own transportation then it can get messy. Don't allow exceptions! This can be a real battle early on, but after the players begin to see how much better they do in matches, then it becomes easier.

2. Warm-up Every Stroke. Players are encouraged to hit a little short court, lengthy ground stroke warm-up, some volleys, and overheads. When there is much more time available I will have my players run a few laps, and do 5-10 stretching exercises.

3. All players do a **full five minutes of serving** warm up. If introductions are at 3:30 PM, then I like everyone on the team to begin at 3:20 PM with their serves. This is just enough to warm up the shoulder. At exactly 3:19, I call to my team to announce that they should begin serving, because it may take a full minute for them to get organized. I attribute my team's ability to start fast with five full minutes of serving. Rarely does the opposition do a full five minute serve warm up.

4. Just prior to introductions, we have a quick five minute meeting with reminders of tactics for the day and **"The Mantra"**.

5. Players lined up for the beginning of introductions **prior to 3:30 p.m**. If the other team is scrambling and trying to get organized while we look and feel totally together, that gives us the mental edge.

6. **Don't** allow an opposing coach to **rush** you or your players into starting before the correct time, unless of course you have made a prior arrangement.

Post-Match--The Day after the Match

I like to talk a bit about the previous day's match, and highlight mainly the best performances, and one or two things to improve, but not name the people who need to improve.

Rarely do I ever give a stern evaluation. At times I have told my team that we won the previous day, but it felt like a loss because we were so ill prepared, or the effort was not championship quality.

I can count on one hand how many times in 26 seasons of coaching that I have immediately after a match disciplined my team. I once made my team run spider runs on the courts of our opponents in full view of that other team. It was a lot like the scene from the movie "Miracle" where Herb Brooks makes the US Hockey Team do intense conditioning after a game. In 2015 I had such a talk with my team after a very lackluster effort, and disinterested cheering for teammates. I let the team know that I was very disappointed with how they let down and lost a match that was winnable. The team responded extremely well, and showed great character for the remainder of the season. I was very proud of their competitiveness to the very end.

99% of the time, it's best to find the positives and build on those. When you put your main focus on improvement, and actively praise those who are improving the most, there is an unspoken motivation. You may want to consider spreading the attention around, so that you are not highlighting the same players over and over.

The lessons learned from playing the matches are the strongest ones you can latch onto, so be sure to seize on them.

CHAPTER FIFTY-THREE
Player Management and Planning

"I coach everyone the same, differently." ~*John Wooden*

It's important to give each player the same amount of care and attention as much as possible. Many times a coach is alone in their responsibility with a very large number of players. There also may be teams divided into varsity and junior varsity with their own coach. Of course, the varsity coach will spend the most time and attention on his top group, but be sure you give attention to everyone in the program. Let your assistants and captains know that if a particular kid is having a problem, to discuss that with you, to make sure you are fully aware of what is going on with that player. Your players may appreciate that you strive to treat them equally, but in reality it's impossible to do this precisely. Even so, be committed to this aspect of coaching, and over time you will gain the trust and admiration of your players. In the short term, there can be some misunderstandings, as some youngsters might not know why you treat one player differently than another. In the mind of a teenager it can be seen as playing favorites.

A girl's team I was coaching had numerous players with 'made up' excuses for missing practice, coming late to practice, and asking for special favors. It started with two varsity girls who were showing a lack of commitment and integrity. Even as I worked with those two trying to get them to buy into what we were doing, the attitudes they brought with them began to spread to other players--more kids were missing practice or coming late.

After a period of a couple of weeks and increasing regularity of the discussion with team captains about commitment, I finally asked the team captains to consider having a team-only meeting. "Please ask this group how good they want to be. Do they want to be excellent and do well in the post-season or just win another league championship and be happy with an early playoff loss? In addition, if they choose the easy route, I will back off from putting the team through some of the more rigorous training in practice, and cease to be so demanding on commitment. I get the feeling they won't like that. I kept hearing complaints that the former coach was not doing enough."

At the end of a practice, we stopped 20 minutes early, the captains lead the meeting, and I heard later that there had been a lot of discussion, tears, apologies offered to one another, then a renewed commitment. That team went on to win it's first round match for the first time in years, in upset fashion. Next up came the #2 seeds. Our girls played out their minds, with one of our captains in the pivotal match winning in a third set tiebreaker. Even though I was extremely proud of their performance, the fact of the matter was that the team was emotionally spent at that point, from the late season drama, and two tough playoff victories. They ran out of mental and emotional gas for the semi-finals and we lost to a young talented team. The lesson was still in play however as at the end of the season, I summed up our season as being 'out of balance', and that if the girls next year could bring a more balanced lifestyle and a greater commitment to what they do, then the sky's the limit. I was not the coach the next year, when they won a sectional title, coming in as the #2 seed themselves, beating the #1 seed in the final. Graciously, the new coach of that team thanked me for instilling the work ethic that fueled them to a sectional title. The team that had been happy to win a league title more often than not, and lose in the first round, would become champions of a higher order.

Just as I am telling you stories here, become a storyteller so that your players can see the values that you want them to aspire to in real-life examples. When I tell stories about players and teams, there is a subconscious message for players as they know that their story may be told one day. They will want to be remembered in the future along with the other great stories. The trick is to keep the retelling very short and give only essential details, when I see the eyes glossing over and rolling, then I know my story is going on too long. Tell stories on rainy days when it's practical, although in some schools it's not practical, because there is no space available to a team for a rainy day. We are educators. It is our duty to teach kids, through sports, how to become better people and better teammates sharing those moments when someone made a breakthrough empowers your players to do the same. Rarely will you have the opportunity to work with a future pro player, but you daily have an opportunity to mold character for a lifetime. It's the story of our lives.

CHAPTER FIFTY-FOUR
Rainy Days

For many teams, rainy days are a huge disappointment because there will be no tennis that day. For some teams its a huge relief for the same reason. I like to get the kids together for an indoor workout, white board 'chalk talk' strategy session, and mental game session, followed by a rousing game of Jeopardy.

In Jeopardy, there will be a category for what they just learned in the workout, the strategy, and the mental game. In addition, there will be a category of Team History so they earn 100 points for something this season, 200 for last season, 500 for something in the last four years, and 1,000 for the annals of greatness from the school. And yes, I have been able to do this at a last place school that had previously won a title.

Jeopardy Categories

Team History, This Years Team, Pro Tennis Trivia

Rules of the Game, Strategy and Tactics, History of Tennis

Mental Game, Weird Stuff Coach Says

The players have fun saying "Weird Stuff Coach Says for 1,000"!

CHAPTER FIFTY-FIVE

Getting Your Team to the Net

Getting Your Players and Teams to the Net: A System to Increase Player Comfort Level

Why Don't Players Come to the Net?
Because they actively fear, or at least have a very low comfort level with:
1. The Possibility of Making a Mistake
2. Getting Hit by the Ball
3. Getting passed clean
4. Not having enough time

One of the major objectives of great coaching is to help inspire confidence and raise the affective filter, and reducing player's anxiety about going forward to the net. This progression from a recent talk I gave to USPTA NorCal Division can really help. As always If you have questions let me know.

Drill One Day One
Approach/Volley with Little or No Discussion or Criticism.
Two Lines   FH DL Approach - BH or Inside Out FH Approach > Volley

Tip: Look for signs of increased comfort moving forward.
5 to 10 minutes

Drill Two Day One
Approach/Volley with discussion about making a great approach
Tip: Take note of improving accuracy of approach
How to Hit a Target
5 to 10 minutes

Drill Three Day Two? (Coach and Players Guide the Progression)
Approach/Volley with Volley Instruction
Aggressive Volleying to Targets
Tip: Reward winning volleys, don't pick on mistakes.
10 to 20 minutes

Drill Four Day Two?
'Rule the Court'
Approaching player must be inside the service box before the point is won.
Tip: Create urgency at moving forward.
First to win 3 points

Drill Five Day Three
Play Set Tiebreakers (7 points)
Server gets ONE serve, Returner must come to the net. No Lobs (Inside the service boxes)
Tip: Stay with it, the first TBs will be ugly, ugly, ugly
This step tests your will, and the comfort of players
Question: "How did it feel to have one serve and know that your next shot would have to be a passing   shot?"   Do you want your opponent to feel that way? YES!
Continue in a round robin with groups of four, play 3 TBs.

Drill Five Day Four

Play Match TBs (10 Points)

Server gets TWO serves, Returner must come to net on second serve. No Lobs.

Tip: Players need to be decisive, realizing its a second serve and they know the plan.

Question: "Did that make you want to take better care of your first serve to make it harder for the   other player to come in?"

Drill Six Day Five

Play a set players who successfully make contact with the ball cannot lose the point. If you come to   the net and touch the ball, you play the point over again, unless you win the point.

Tip: Bridge the 'making contact' with urging players to get in position for better volleys.

This step has a greater challege level.

Drill Seven Day Six

Play a set, players who win the point at net get three points. The player need not make a   volley, but they must be inside a service box at the time the point is one.

Idea: Have a player chart the win/loss % of points, and/or tally up how points were won or lost. Passing Shot Error, Volley Winner, Volley Error, Passing Shot Winner is the possible order depending on level of play. You may find: Passing Shot Error, Volley Winner, Passing Shot Winner, Volley Error among higher level players.

For higher level teams: Emphasize having passing shot artists make sure the volleyer must play. Do not go for too much on a first passing shot attempt. Simply stretch out your opponent, open the court and go for a pass on the next ball. Accidental passing shot winners are acceptable.

To book me to speak or to ask a question about these notes send me an email bill@pattonschooloftennis.com

CHAPTER FIFTY-SIX
Visualization and Self Talk

Visualization

Another rainy day activity is to spend some time visualizing. Taking the time to help players learn and experience progressive relaxation, and then visualization can help them quite a bit in their young lives. Many teenagers live anxiety riddled lives, so helping them to become more calm, not only helps them on court, but also in academics and in relationships. I have an audio file I will gladly share with you if you join my email list. It contains scripts for guiding your team in visualization for different lengths of times. I lead my team to visualize the great feelings that come with winning a league title, beating the team above us in the standings, or getting that first league win of the year. Not every player loves doing this, but I do enforce that everyone must keep their eyes closed.

Prior to visualizing, I may show them some videos of a particular stroke or pattern that I want them to learn.

While they get into a light trance state, I will also ask them how do our strokes look? How do we look after we make a mistake? After one or maybe two good long sessions, we stop for a moment during practice and visualize for a minute or two. It's a great thing to do when the performance of a task is not matching up with how we want it to look.

Self Talk

Players some times talk themselves into bad play. Perhaps the most common thought problem players have is when they are about to hit a second serve. They may say to themselves "Don't Double Fault", which leads directly to a high percentage of double faults. Replacing a thought like that with "Make a serve deep to the backhand corner" is an effective way to direct your mind back to what you want and eliminate the fear of missing. Of course, there is no guarantee that you won't ever double fault, but the chances decrease dramatically if you don't use the words 'double fault' prior to serving. This is just one example of ways people say things to themselves that will cause them to make mistakes. As a coach interview your players to find out what kinds of thoughts they have while they play. It doesn't have to become psychotherapy, but you might be surprised by some of the things going on with your players. Sometimes they are scared of their opponent.

CHAPTER FIFTY-SEVEN
Revenge Served Cold

One player that I nicknamed Chi Chi, because her family had Chihuahuas as pets, also had a feisty personality similar to those little pooches. Chi Chi would have a great opportunity to 'bite back'. We were at a team tournament, and one of our freshman players was crouching near the fence to pull a ball out of the fence. Her opponent seemed to seize that moment of vulnerability to return the other ball at 60 mph aimed at her head, but she presumably was 'just giving the ball back'. I could see the intent in her eyes to intimidate my player. We had already witnessed something similar in a previous match. At that time, I had instructed that coach about the action taken by her player. That coach issued her own player a code violation-warning. In our area it was becoming something USTA junior girls did to try to intimidate one another. The ball missed my young player's head by just a few feet, and I saw the whole thing developing. The other player did not show any remorse for frightening my player. I became very upset with this act of poor sportsmanship.

I started a bit of a ruckus, as I was indignant about the act, and I was not going to sit idly by, while this happened again to one of my players. To make a long story short, the head coach of the other team took care of the matter in his own due time. We lost the match against a very strong team. This one act of poor sportsmanship however created fuel for my team, as they felt very good about the way I defended them. It can be noted that the fervor with which I defended my girl with the other coach was not lost on my team. Some of the girls later told me that they felt I was their protector, and it helped them feel comfortable. But, thats not where this story ends.

We made it to the post-season, and pulled a first round upset, then we moved into the second round against this same team which was a #2 seeded. Our team was seeded #10 and we had already dramatically defeated the #7 seed in the first round. In the first encounter, the young lady that was the offender had beaten my #1 player Chi Chi, in routine fashion. Somehow, I knew there would be no need to provide any motivation for this match. Chi Chi became very quiet and like a ferocious Chihuahua she attacked her opponent relentlessly winning 6-0, 6-0 in one of most dominant performances against a #1 player I have ever seen. The other girl was helpless in the match and afterward she cried. Our girl had taken her game to a new level with full motivation for a revenge that was served cold, as per the directions. We emerged victorious 4-3 in a very closely contested match, that the entire team wanted very badly given what had happened previously. That decisive victory was an enormous confidence boost for the whole team. A word of caution: there was no way to predict that Chi Chi was going to play that great. When players play with a sense of revenge, sometimes they try to play a game that they don't own, they might try to play super human tennis, only to make many more mistakes than they normally do. So, serve that revenge cold!

CHAPTER FIFTY-EIGHT
Teenagers and Balanced Lifestyle

Many high school kids have the idea they can do it all. I'm solidly with Wayne Bryan when he says if you have school, a sport, and a fine art and they need to be in that order, even if the fine art is above the sport then you have enough on your plate that you can pursue with excellence. Unfortunately, many teenagers pursue planned mediocrity, but overcommitting themselves to too many activities, and the effect is that they don't do any of them with excellence.

I demand a commitment to the team and encourage the youngsters to make good decisions about how they use their time. With very few exceptions, I do not allow players to skip practice because they may have fallen behind in academics. Currently I am coaching at a school that has numerous players who really do struggle mightily with academics, so I have developed a new policy that a player can skip one practice for academics, but they have to communicate this too me ahead of time. After those two are used up, then missing practice falls under team consequences. Letting them off easy will teach them that commitment is not important to me or to them. At the conclusion of one season with a girl's team I was quite fond of, I felt I needed to include a "what we learned" summary at our end of the year banquet. Those girls were very energetic and accomplished a lot, but many of them also became ill and reached the wall of exhaustion especially after the insane schedule they kept during spirit week, when everyone was up well after midnight working on floats, skits and decorations. After two very thrilling playoff wins, that team was spent, and we could do nothing in the semi-finals of the section championship. I had left coaching at that school prior to the next year, and to hear their next coach tell it, the groundwork for a section championship had been laid in the previous year. He was gracious enough to extend a thank-you to me, and I am very proud of those girls who I assume took on a more balanced lifestyle.

CHAPTER FIFTY-NINE
When to Listen to Your Team

It was late in the season, and my team looked a little tired. On the schedule things lined up nicely for us to have a good day of conditioning, making it our last push before some big matches in the coming weeks. I gathered my three captains: Peter, the voted and undisputed team captain; Aaron, the soft-spoken leader by example, but high energy athlete; and Vincent, the academic guy who seemed to wear down at the end of each season. I asked these three whether we should have a tough conditioning day, then finish with a fun game, or whether we should have a light practice and play a lot of fun large group games (the way I run them, they *do offer fitness*).

Peter said "Sure, let's make it tough", like a dutiful captain who can also stand to lose some weight. Aaron got a cruel look in his eye, and said, "Yes, tough", as though he wanted everyone to be tortured and he was going to love it. Vincent said, "Coach, I'm wiped out, and there are few guys that are feeling the same way," I said, "Okay, guys, it's 2-1. So what do you think we are going to do?" They all thought we would have a tough practice. I then said, "Let this be a lesson to you. 'Majority rules' is not the best way to lead a group. If you run the risk of pushing people over a cliff from which they will not recover, then back away from the cliff. Sometimes the decisions you make are about respecting the lack of capacity, and a need for rest that will make you more successful. Thank you to Vincent for being honest in the face of what seemed certain to be a tough practice. Today, we are going to take it easy, because I don't want Vincent and a handful of other players exhausted as we head into the home stretch run." It turned out to be exactly what we needed to have the energy to finish our miracle run to a shared championship.

CHAPTER SIXTY
Listening v. Maintaining the Plan

I have a simple rule, because teenagers can act like impulsive puppies and we need to give them a steady hand of leadership. They will come to you and ask, "Can we do such and such today (something fun)?" it will come across as urgent begging with a lying promise of approval. Don't cave. My rule is that the first answer is always "NO!". I can always then think about it and change my mind, but it's best early in the season NOT to do what they ask on the same day they ask it.

I like to say, "Okay, I have my plan already set for today, so let's see if we can work that in on a future day. What is it? Oh, I'm so sorry, I don't really see the value in it for a practice, but how about we do that on one of our goof-off days right after a tough match."

I always have an easy, fun day planned for the day after we face our toughest test of the league season. I also let my players know that, win or lose, we are still going to have fun and play games tomorrow, so don't worry about me punishing you tomorrow. This also empowers my players to go all-out during these tough matches, knowing we are not going to be conditioning the next day.

CHAPTER SIXTY-ONE
Conspiracy Clique

One season, J and M had been running a game, acting like petulant NBA superstars who think they can manipulate the team and run it their way. They were skipping practices, making excuses, breaking team rules, and not following up on consequences handed out to them. This was having a negative effect on their teammates, as it seemed that these two were too cool to hang out with the guys on our team. It all came to a head because those two were not really part of the team; they held themselves separate and above the others. After a tough loss against our main rivals, which put us in a tough position, facing an uphill climb to try to win a league title, M quit the team. The timing of this was very poor, and also it was seemed rather sudden, just prior to the due date for our team's selections to the league tournament team for the end of the season. M did not give much in the way of specific reasons for quitting.

My team captain got wind of a story that M and J had conspired, figuring that J would get the singles spot vacated by M, which seemed like a logical assumption. In close talks with my captains, I decided that the consequence for not following up with team rules, and the consequences of breaking them was that J would not be selected to the league tournament. The next day at practice I announced the post season squad team, and it took J about 45 seconds of shock to realize his name was not on it. He immediately marched out of practice.

As he got closer to the fence, I announced that if he left the court then he would be suspended from the team. He is still suspended from the team, despite the best efforts of his mother to convince me that I am stubborn and should not have so many rules. When he left the gate, I shouted, "I guess you never really have been a team player," It seemed like such a horrible end to a tough season, as we lost some matches we most likely would have won otherwise. My colleagues who were the coaches of rival teams took the time to point out how I had lost some good players from my team. Thanks guys! A funny thing happened, though. The team became much happier within days of our team 'cancer surgery'. Those two were making the rest of the team so miserable it had affected their preparation and play all season long. Our team captain won a league title, and did well at sectionals, partly fueled by the desire to end well. While our team was weakened with losing the #2 and #4 players on the team, everyone below stepped up their game. This all set the tone for...

CHAPTER SIXTY-TWO
"A" Redeems the Situation

A had become the new team captain for the season, having been a quiet leader as a co-captain the year before. He approached me about the possibility of M returning to the team because M was his friend. I said, "Normally, if someone quits, I would never trust them again, so I don't know if it would work. But if you want to follow up on this, I will allow you to do it. M will have to make a firm commitment to the team."

In the weeks leading up to the season A, M, and myself had numerous talks. I did not want to make it very easy, however I knew the team would have a good chance at a fairly successful season with M playing #1 and probably have a very tough season without him. Interestingly enough, M was helping coach in a nearby program for younger kids who needed help.

He offered to come every time he could, but I rejected that. The deal was, he had to be at every practice and ready to play or be at none of them. Whatever we did, it was going to be all or nothing, as it would not be fair to the team to show him weekly special favors. I said, "I don't want to wonder on a daily basis if you're coming, and it's a distraction to the team if you're there one day and not there the next. Also, if you miss one match without notice, then you'll be off the team. Here is a list of matches you must play."

It seemed to work quite well, and even though it was not comfortable for me to make an exception to policy, he kept his part of the bargain. There was only one player on the team that was unhappy with the arrangement, but he had his own issues. M went out of his way to engage his teammates, and he actively cheered their matches when his was done. I was very pleased with his presence on the team. Further, he notified me early that he would not be able to play the post-season singles tournament, which allowed me to prepare another player, who then pulled a huge upset and it culminated his career on a strong positive note.

Consider for a moment if I did not allow him back onto the team. A positive experience of reconciliation would have been lost to us all, and our team would not have won a share of a championship. Championships are rare birds to be cherished, especially in the face of great adversity.

CHAPTER SIXTY-THREE
The Prima Donna

Parents and players, how would you like the effect you or your child have on a tennis team to be remembered forever as a huge negative? I would hope not. I had just begun coaching at a school that was extremely weak and in danger of not having a season if I had not stepped up to coach, which is not something I want to brag about, but it shows how dire the situation was. Ironically, there was a girl coming in as a freshman who was a nationally ranked USTA junior player. Knowing full well that no one on the team could hit two balls with her, I knew she would need some type of special arrangement if she were going to play. I was ready and willing to discuss it with her or her parents.

School had started, and she had not yet reported to the team. Which made her about two weeks late to practice. I asked the AD to have her come visit with me, or I could visit her at school. I had made around 10 attempts to get through to this young lady with no response from her. Then, just 24 hours before our first league match of the season was to begin, she came to talk to me. I let her know to be at the match against the first-place team the next day.

She arrived about five minutes prior to the match, and I handed her a uniform. She went to put it on, came back, played her match, beat last years league champion 6-0,6-0. Then she came to inform me defiantly with hands on hips, and from her 14-year-old mouth, "I will only be playing the home matches." So I casually said, "OK, it's over, turn in your uniform because that was your only match. Congratulations you just beat the reigning league champion."

What followed was way too much discussion, and negotiation between me, the girl, her parents, the athletic director, and the principal of the school. It was discovered that the principal had made the girl the the same deal that it had made for a now famous olympic ice skating champion. That ice skater had gone to the same school district, and she had a special deal not to take PE classes and do some classes as independent study. Ultimately, an agreement was made that this player would also play only the home matches. I was not informed of this arrangement until it was too late, presumably to do anything about it. We went forward with allowing her to only attend the matches, all matches. However, she began to give lame excuses to avoid playing matches she did not want to play.

Interestingly, during that season we broke the team's 71-match losing streak. Even though this girl was a great player, she still only accounted for one win. It was truly a great team effort from the rest of the girls that mad it happen. Having the Prima Donna on the team only helped with better match ups on the day. After that happened, I contacted local media. We got some special write-ups in the newspaper, and I worked to try to get us featured on network TV. The local high school sports weekly TV show decided to have us on, so they were coming to our next match for a brief interview before start of our next match. I agreed.

Our prima donna called me with another lame excuse to miss the match, which was okay, because then she would have to miss being on TV. My team captains were absolutely incredible in their interviews, and our team was featured as "Team in the Spotlight" which was the highest honor on a weekly basis.

The following match, the final match of the season, and the Prima Donna would need to play it for to be eligible to play for a league title and have a strong chance at a sectional title. The further along we went, the more I realized she was using our team as a stepping stone to individual glory, no matter the mental and emotional cost to our team. She had skipped the previous match, so I kept her out of the line-up, especially because she had not informed me if her excuse was solved. I was just plain exhausted by the back and forth and weekly negotiations. I called to let her know that she was not going to be in the line-up.

As the matches were just about to start, my phone rang and she pleaded with me to play the match. Next, her father called. We had a 15-minute conversation and some very interesting facts came to light. All this confirmed that she only wanted a league title and a section title in her trophy case. I had heard she went on to play college tennis. My sincere hope is that she learned something about being a team player and made a commitment to getting the most out of it. If she reads or gets wind of this, I would hope that she has matured and finds this somewhat embarrassing and fairly humorous, as I think that some of what she exhibited was some very strong ambition for a 14-year- old girl. She had not had enough training in how to deal with a situation like this one. It's an instructive story for juniors, coaches, and parents about the impact a strong player can have on a team, either positively or negatively.

CHAPTER SIXTY-FOUR
Mistake Management - Perceptions

While a handful of high school players can use pro and college techniques and strategies to win matches, the vast majority of high school players need to focus most in reducing the amount of mistakes they make in a match. Reducing errors is one thing, and taking calculated risks is another, but in reality every shot has some amount of risk attached to it. I never use the word "consistent" with my players, as it the idea they should never make a mistake. The work consistent is almost never used in a positive light to evaluate a match. So we begin by understanding that everyone is going to make multiple mistakes, and we want to strategize to reduce them.

A phenomenal performance on hard courts is when you have one winner for every error you make. A strong match for many high school players is one winner for every two errors made. For players that lack the power to hit winners, they must focus more on reducing those. Sometimes a player has five errors for every winner. It's much more realistic to reduce errors than it is to suddenly increase the amount of winners.

When helping players to begin reducing errors, I start with early recognition of the incoming ball. Players may get a little lazy about seeing the ball, and then all their reactions are late and lack precision. If a player really simply scans to the other side to be aware of the opponent's contact point of where the ball and racket meet, it could solve the problem. Another way to address this is to have the player take shorter backswings to allow them to play more error free, as this can help them to time the ball more easily. As they gain confidence they can reach back for a bit more on the ball.

Psychologically, I want my players to be aware of their errors and not worried that I hate all errors. Errors long are good, since you are getting good depth. We talk a lot about the risk:reward ratio, and how you have to take some risks to gain higher percentages of points won.

Another mental aspect of mistake management is when players look to see if their coach saw the error. That's a great time to give a disapproving look! Haha, just kidding! I like to look away instantly from a match where my player made a mistake, and I know they are relieved because they think I didn't see it. Generally, I start a quick conversation with the person next to me. Sometimes I pretend like I need to go to another location on-site.

Help players accept mistakes, then learn to objectively see how they are making them, discover the most common mistake they make and fix that one first. You can swing the match in the other direction if your players are not worried about mistakes, but are managing the risk:reward ratio.

CHAPTER SIXTY-FIVE
Miracles Happen - Beating MV

As I was planning my year with the best team I have ever coached, I decided it would be great to put it all on the line, creating the strongest season schedule I had assembled in all of my years of coaching. Since I knew this team would need to be very well-prepared for post-season and could handle a few losses without losing confidence, I called all the toughest teams I could find took my team to a tough tournament and held a tournament of our own.

One particular team I wanted to play was a perennial section champion and finalist. They had won our section the most times since sectional team play was established. I called the coach what seemed like 20 times. At some point during the process of scheduling this match, I wrote, "Beat MV" on a label and fastened that label on my calendar where I would see every day.

I was disappointed that the match was never scheduled, but I knew there was a chance we could face this team at an invitational or in the section playoffs, so I left it there. In my mind it seemed like a dream, because I didn't think it was very likely. If we played them, more than one player would have to play out of their minds, and that team would have to weaken themselves somehow for us to win.

I stared at that sticker for five months. I trained my team to the very edge of what they might be capable of and prepared for that one win that may never come. In our realistic outcome goals for the season, we set the goal of gaining at least second place in our section to make the NorCal Regional Championships, which is as far as you can go in California, because we don't have a state championship in tennis. Two things came up as our season went along: we began to play extremely good doubles, and our team unity was extremely good because of a threat posed from within our team. Everyone on our team had to pull together to meet the threat. Favorably for us, I had heard that MV was having team chemistry issues. They had a player who had transferred to their school, and presumably his presence in the #2 spot behind a D1 college prospect made them untouchable.

Let's move ahead to the time when we are winning our semifinal in the section, and now assuring ourselves a place in NorCals. We were made aware that the same #2 player from MV had decided to play a large junior tournament for his own ranking, and that their team was still very confident they could beat us without him that it was not a cause for concern. It was a great day for the #2 player on our team to play out of his mind, and make great tactical adjustments, and also for two of my doubles players on separate teams to do the same. My #1 doubles team was nearly unbeatable, so we swept doubles and won one singles match for the win in come-from-behind fashion.

Earlier in the day we had defeated the #2 seeds by a 5-2 score, even as one of our doubles teams played poorly. It was now 97 degrees, and we were facing the #1 seeded team, down 3 matches to 1. We were down one set in one match and had split sets in two others. We needed to win the remaining four sets on court to win the match. At a critical juncture with all the fans of the #1 team licking their chops, expecting victory at any moment. During a lull in play, one fan yelled out "Go Warriors!" at the top of his lungs. From then, onward you could sense a surge of effort and confidence from the Warriors, as they laid all their effort on the line to come from behind for a 4-3 victory to seize the section title. The #3 seeds defeated #2, and #1 in the same day, in difficult heat to win!

CHAPTER SIXTY-SIX
Types of Teams

Championship Caliber Team

There is very little drop off in ability from position to position on great teams, and more than one good player does not make varsity. The highest level teams actually cut players from the JV who can play tennis, due to space constraints. With a team at this level, I recommend having no more than a 4:1 ratio of players on the team to courts. Otherwise, players become bored with having to share court time. I have taken up to 26 players for 6 courts, but then I let the last 6 players know that they will be sharing a court quite often and make the best of it. With a team like this, it should run almost like a college program. Teaching the subtleties of how to win a match, tweaking slightly a stroke and there, adding a weapon, or enhancing a weapon with more tactics.

Strong Team

This type of team probably has some very strong players at the top and minimal drop-off on the varsity team, but will lose to the championship level team due to depth. JV players may have fundamental flaws, and there are some beginners that, come out for the team. Your job is to prepare your varsity first, get them into a routine, then go and fix a few flaws, while sprinkling in some beginner lessons for the new players. It's a mistake to take too much time preparing the beginners and fixing the JV players. That's a job that must wait until the varsity is in a bit of a groove and adjusted to season routines.

Aspiring Team

It's good to know how motivated the players are on your team. If they aspire to be great, then take the time to teach them how to play. The short term results might not be great, but you should help them realize their capabilities at the end of the season, and try to make it a springboard for future seasons. The key with a team like this is to show them championship level teams and how those players prepare themselves for their tennis careers that most likely extend beyond high school play.

Not So Good Team

Blow it up and start over. Work to create a completely new culture. Start with principles from this book, and don't look back. The program may shrink while you create critical mass of a group of caring players. Teach, teach, teach. When you change the culture, you will find that a new group of players will be attracted to the program, more ambitious players.

CHAPTER SIXTY-SEVEN
Understanding Performance

Perhaps the most important thing that I wish I had known, when I got started coaching is not to put pressure on players before, during, or after matches. Ultimately players choose if they are going to take on pressure, as it's an internal choice. But if you are not offering it to them, they are much less likely to choose it. Recently a large case study showed that when elite athletes feel pressure they report that they perform more poorly.

One of the ways I have put pressure on my players is in the way I evaluate matches. Once I heard Dick Gould, 18-time NCAA National Champion coach say, "First question I ask the players is, 'Did you have fun?'" Prior to hearing that, I spent too much time suggesting that the player or team 'had to' play great today. We really 'need' this win. Now, I almost never give special advice, but settled into the mantra and began to ask kids if they had fun. Of course, having come off the court playing a very good or great match, I would be sure to notice and praise them or acknowledge with empathy that they had a tough day on court. What goes on the mind of a youngster when they know their coach is interested first in their fun, then in the result of the match. It's always harder inside the fence, especially when you have a lot of teenage fears running around in your head.

Winning-streaks are dangerous if you don't already have a built-in philosophy for how to handle them. When a team becomes successful at a much higher rate in terms of wins and losses, the next thing they do is become overconfident. It's nearly a spring loaded situation that teams that are successful at a new level, are prone to fall into trap games against lesser opponents.

You can work with your team captains and prepare them, so you can criticize them during the streak. Challenge the captain to improve, especially if he or she has lost or had sub- par performances during the streak. Of course, you need a mature captain for that. If you have a player who happens to be on a hot streak, acknowledge it after it becomes quite lengthy. If you build up the excitement of the streak, then it pressurizes it moving forward.

M, was on a bad streak. His father was a real task master. M had been the #1 player the year before I arrived to coach the team, which coincided with the arrival of a very talented freshman player who would vie for the top spot. I wanted their challenge match to occur as quickly as possible.

After a few days in practice, when everyone was looking fairly good, M played the hot shot. That produced a 6-1 win for the hot shot. They played again in a few days, 6-0 for the hot shot. M was now #2 on the team. It was important to get that done quickly so M would have time to cope. M moped around for a bit, and in the coming days he started to show some behavior problems for a very short while.

Soon, the #3 player had been working extremely hard on his game, and wanted to challenge M. A 6-4 later win and #3 became #2. M was then the #3 player, and looking like he wanted someone to give him something for free. M played poorly in the #3 position, playing down to the level of some pre-season competition, and lost a winnable match. Finally, there is a blow up, when he and a friend were goofing around at practice, wasting time, and distracting teammates, as they were hitting balls over the fence. I went crazy, confronting M, I really laid into him and let him know that he is talented and ought not to waste his talent. As he was nearly reduced to tears, I stopped, softened my voice and told him quietly. "Hey, the reason I just did that was because I care. I care what happens with you, and I think you are a good player who can do much better", or something along those lines. We eventually worked it out, and M started to play better.

The focus of this story is to bring attention to how players can become disappointed with their status on the team. M's father came to a match, and was quite angry with M during the match. I asked him to please be quiet as he was also disturbing other matches, I then took a very comical posture for M and during a changeover asked him to keep his eyes on me and not his father. This seemed to break the pattern of negativity and pressure. M's bad streak quickly became a good streak, he regained his #2 spot, and nearly regained the #1 spot, barely missing out, but now he was able to accept that the other player deserved it. M finished his high school experience winning 21 of the last 22 matches in his career. However, I knew that I could not get too excited during the early phases. M went on to play college tennis and also later on a National Champion USTA Team. Experiencing a lengthy success streak can facilitate future successes.

E was a team captain, and had been practicing very hard. He also put a lot of pressure on himself to be a good example to the team so we could all be successful. E also was leading some fellow players that were not keen on his leadership, which in my mind was *their* problem. E went into a real funk and his game kept getting worse and worse. He would play a match, do poorly with a stroke or strategy, we would work on that in the next practice, and then he would go and play even more poorly. It was a complete mystery, so I asked to see his racket. He was using synthetic strings that not only were strung way too tight, but also had not been replaced since the year before! I strung his racket and his game took off, and there was joy in the kingdom. The point here is remember to take care of your equipment and your strings are perhaps the most important piece.

M was a feisty girl and prone to stubbornness. She was on a streak, but I wanted to make sure she kept building new facets to her game. I would work with her on a certain shot, then she would do it one time and almost intentionally lose the point, and then say, "I told you it wouldn't work!" Over a period of time, she adopted a new tactic. She was winning close matches. M was probably the third best player in league, and her battles with #4 were awesome, each going three long sets. M gained the edge as she adopted two new plays in her game prior to their league tournament encounter. M got off to a blazing start mixing tactics well and hitting winners all over the place. She was up 3-0 before you could blink. When it was 5-0, the opposing coach was taking a long time on the changeover, so I felt obligated to talk to M as well. "I'm here to say hi. I like what you are doing; keep going." If I had taken time to say any more than that, I ran the risk of getting M thinking about what I said instead of doing what she was doing. She won 6-0, 6-0 against the player she had beaten 7-5 in the third two previous times, hitting maybe 30 winners and less than 5 unforced errors. It was quite an incredible display. The point is to keep working new things into your player's game, even if they are winning regularly, and respect the 'out of their mind' performance by not coaching.

R was a top 30 ranked sectional USTA junior until he hit high school. By then, he was already burnt out on USTA play, got into his team play, and focused on being valedictorian. His first season with the team, he came in lights out and came from Court 8 on Day 1, to Court 2 on Day 2, and then on Day 3 Court 1 was his for the rest of the next two seasons. His second year, he came into the season looking rusty because he was not playing tournaments all the time. Players on the team were worried, and yet I knew he would be fine. Since he had been a league finalist in his first year, everyone assumed he would always look great. This is when you need to have steady hand and be patient. I talked to R about making sure he came to the matches early enough to warm up. At that point I also started with an expectation that everyone on the team would be on-court 30 minutes prior to the start of a match. I wanted to know that they had spent around 20 minutes hitting every shot, and R was my reason for this. After about three weeks in, R was fine and maybe better than before and went on to win the league singles title.

CHAPTER SIXTY-EIGHT
Planning a Move or Two Ahead in Years

In planning over years there are some factors to help you decide how to proceed. I hope you are reading this because, you plan to coach for many years and want to build a cohesive program, where year to year the players understand how the program works. Ideally, you have a great team, and there is an established system of 'waiting your turn' to become a varsity player or singles player. Even so, extremely talented freshmen and sophomores do emerge, and they are great for the continuity of the program. Here are some questions I ask when I first get started. Who are my seniors? Are they leaders and motivated? Juniors? If you inherited some unmotivated seniors, it might be tough first year. Give them the benefit of the doubt. Always believe they can change their minds, but, "There is a time to seek, and a time to give up as lost" is a proverb that sadly comes into play as some times you work with a player and they simply don't want it. That's when I go to a stronger junior leader, and begin the dialogue about what I am doing to prepare for the next year. Sometimes, unmotivated seniors can be the worst kind of cancer on your team. If you expect players to ascend to certain levels, then it is possible to give them a taste of that this year. Who are my hard-working players who are freshmen and sophomores? Promote them and give attention to them, not necessarily to the more talented players.

CHAPTER SIXTY-NINE
Stories of Pivotal Choices

B and J

We had fairly large team with over 40 players to begin on 8 courts. Over time, kids quit the team because they did not want to work very hard. Eventually, we would finish the season with around 28 players. In their first year on the team, B and J were constantly at the bottom, finishing as #27 and #28 on the ladder. However, they always worked hard, almost never complained, and come to the program I ran in the summer. Having played all summer and into the fall, when spring came around they had improved dramatically. On the first day of practice for the spring, I announced, "Gentlemen, we are going to start by watching B and J hit some balls." One player sarcastically responded, "Why would we want to do that?" "Just wait," I said.

So Ben and Jun rallied and immediately I could see the look of terror on the eyes of those who had not put in much work, as they realized they most likely had been passed on the ladder. This motivated some players to ramp up their effort levels. Eventually, Ben and Jun both played varsity and had a very fulfilling tennis experience.

T and M

Once I had two co-captains who decided they were going to do everything possible at school in their senior year. They would have made a fine #2 or #3 doubles team, but they skipped practices or were preoccupied with the school play, school government, club leadership, etc. After some talks about what was best, I helped both of them to see and decide not to play on the team. At first, they were shocked, and thought it to mean that I did not like them. The team was also shocked when they left. We chose new captains quickly, and went on to have a fine season. The groundwork for a higher level of commitment was laid, and the next season we won our first title in 26 years. We started a 6-year run where no team in the league had a better record than us over that span. All this from a program that had hovered around .500 with some bad years sprinkled in. To this day I owe T and M a debt of gratitude for realizing what they were doing and making their school year better by not creating 10 weeks of misery. Recently, I reconnected with T who thanked me for a valuable lesson learned, one that he applies in his life now in his early thirties.

CHAPTER SEVENTY
Coaching Boys and Girls

Every year I am accused of being much nicer to the girls. After the boys have been on my team, then they watch how I deal with the girls, they feel jealous. But each group has different needs.

I sure hope nothing I say here comes across as sexist, because there is much science to support the idea that men's and women's brains operate generally different. Of course, be careful using generalizations, because there is a fairly wide band of behavior across the continuum.

In general, boys are going to be a bit more competitive and girls a bit more fun. Of course, you will find some not so competitive boys, and some very competitive girls. Girls will tend be more communicative, and boy's less so. Boy's won't want or need to be acknowledged by the coach to the same degree as girls, but also may need that affirmation. These are all generalities because there are always exceptions.

Even so, coaching a boy's team and a girl's team can quite different.

Boy's - I find it necessary to challenge the boys and keep them challenged from the beginning, until they naturally can go through practice with a higher level of self discipline.

Get right to work, conditioning to the full measure of their capacity

Boy's will respond to a high challenge level more quickly than girls in general.

Girl's - They don't care how much you know, until they know how much you care. It's wise to test out a certain challenge level, check to see if they are over or underwhelmed then adjust the challenge level accordingly. It will be important to make sure you learn the girls names as quickly as possible, and also greet them all by name as they enter practice or matches.

Training girls is similar to cooking frogs. Frogs are cooked alive, so its best to put them in a pot of lukewarm water, and slowly increase the heat. Because they are cold blooded creatures they will not notice the slowly increasing heat. If you throw a frog into a hot pot, they will jump right now.

Send me an email for some notes from Dr. Cheryl McLaughlin's great talk on "Male Coaches Coaching Female Athletes".

CHAPTER SEVENTY-ONE
Keeping Sports in Perspective

Certain assumptions we make about organizations or people are that they don't care, they are lazy, or they need to be made to want to win. In management circles, this is called Theory X. When we consider that people are motivated to do what they want to do, it gives us another way to develop them by drawing them out, asking them to want certain things, like a championship or to be a complete player or to buy into the team concept. This is Theory Y where the players already want to win badly enough and they feel pressure not to lose, so adding pressure is counterproductive. For years I have been making a transition from being a Theory Y coach to a Theory Z coach. Theory Z is that people want to engage in activities that will help them develop as life-long learners. The lessons learned on a tennis court can help people in many other areas of life.

In my first meeting with a team, I talk about world history. I put two numbers on the board in the classroom where we have the meeting. Toward the end of the meeting, as we discuss what I expect as a reasonable outcome for the team, I point to the two numbers. The first is 36,000,000. "Do you know what that is?" I ask. That's the number of people who fought and died in the 20th century, in all wars combined. The other number is 100,000,000. "What do you think that is? It's the number of people who may have been killed, kidnapped, jailed, or were never seen again-- in their own country! Stalin is estimated to have killed upwards of 30,000,000 people, according to a history professor at the University of Hawai'i. Why are we talking about this? Because if we go 16-0 and win the section, we don't bring any of those people back. If we go 0-16, we still don't add to the number. So keep in mind--it's not life or death! Now, for the sake of gratitude to those who fought and died, and stand on guard right now to give you this opportunity to play--let's make the most of it." I then never discuss that again, because I trust that they will always remember.

Recently, I interviewed Tennis Legend Torben Ulrich (http://bitly. com/ 1a7PqNQ), take a listen. One thing that came out of that interview is great perspective about the meaning of competition. It's a great privilege to be present and compete, and having the experience of playing with a ball can be a precious time.

Here is a story of a very precious moment indeed. When my team played the California Tennis Classic, the largest high school tennis tournament in the country, we did quite well. We were selected for Division 1, among the 9 divisions, with over 110 teams in the event.

We lost our first match, which put us in flight two of Division 1, which was perfect because we had some very close competition in that group. I knew we would have some tough matches. In flight one, it would have been tough sledding, and we most likely would have finished 4th. My preference was to try to finish 5th and gain some confidence along the way. Unknown to us at the time, the tournament gave nice, long-sleeve t-shirts to every team down to 5th place. Sometimes losing is still winning.

We got into a very tight group and went 2-1. The team we lost to was 2-0, and was going to play a team we beat. It turned out that if a three-way tie occurred, we would win the tie-breaker, based on fewest matches lost. The team to whom we lost, also made many bad calls, and had quite a chip on their shoulders, so it was not a fun match, and it made it much easier to root against them. Having finished 2-1, we were done with our matches, and now we could either drive over three hours home, or we could stay and watch the end of the other match. We could have saved some time, and waited to find out the result on the internet. The tournament could send us our shirts. We didn't know how the third-place team would beat the first-place team, but we went to see anyway.

The match was a good one, and the first place team led 3-2 in matches. But lo and behold, a player came from behind to win a match, and the match was knotted at 3-3. The #3 doubles teams were playing, with the first place team ahead 5-3, and if they broke serve they would win 5th place overall, and the t-shirts we wanted. This is where, with my whole team watching, they were able to see why they should never give up. It was quite remarkable to see how smug and overconfident the first-place team became while up 5-3. Most people relaxed, but then the other team held serve for 5-4, and the first place team got a little tight. Even so, they worked their way to match point, and that's where the "shot that saved the shirt" occurred.

On match point, a player from team #1 hit a deft drop volley that looked for all the world to be unreachable. Suddenly, one player from the challenging team seemed to fly over 20 feet in one second, and used a backhand skillet flipping grip on the forehand side, while less than three feet from the net moving to his right from the doubles alley, flipping left and making less than a 10-degree angled drop shot winner that the #1 team could only watch! Even though it passed within a few feet of them, it was physically impossible for them to react and move to hit it. The ball landed on the opposite doubles sideline for a winner. One of the players had a look on his face that said to me, "*I wish I could call that out, but look there are way too many people in the stands watching.*"

The #1 team was stunned. The match went into a tie-breaker, won by the #3 team, and we got long sleeved t-shirts. That is a precious moment we did not even participate in, but that is exactly the kind of experience we want our players to have--to see the impossible drop shot response winner save the t-shirt. Five years later, I still wear mine. I will never forget the backhand skillet grip forehand extreme angle drop shot for a winner.

CHAPTER SEVENTY-TWO
Reader Today, Leader Tomorrow

Peter Burwash one of the most influential tennis coaches in the history of our sport shared a story of giving President Jimmy Carter tennis lessons. After lesson one he gave Jimmy the gift of three of his books. Jimmy responded by giving Peter his book. Peter said he felt obligated to read some of Jimmy's book, to show appreciation for the gift. So he read ten pages, and went back to the next lesson sharing with Jimmy, "I read ten pages of your book." Jimmy responded, "I read all three of yours; very good, thanks" Peter was stunned. Jimmy shared with Peter, "I had always heard 'reader today, leader tomorrow', so learned how to speed read." Carter was known as one of the few presidents who actually read for himself all the briefings and much of the raw material that is given to a president. The point is not to discuss Jimmy as president, but to show the value of continuing to read up on the game. Right now I am preaching to the choir, no? So keep it up coach!

The Complete Guide to Conditioning for Tennis by the USTA is my favorite book produced by the USTA, maybe the best thing they have produced. It's a cornerstone of my conditioning program. Share with me if you find something more valuable. There are some gems in that book. I still use the spider run, which has been the number one agility drill that I use again and again.

CHAPTER SEVENTY-THREE
Measure Fitness and other Performance

Sometimes we get so complicated in our approach that we never measure to see if, our players are actually become quicker. I decided to use the standards given for what is an average quickness score for a nationally ranked or young professional at 18 years of age for my team. I have my team strive to achieve that level. Initially our goal was to have someone do the spider run in 15.4 seconds or lower. In 1999, I had two players who performed the spider run under 16 seconds. My number one player had a 15.4 time. In 2000, my goal was to have the entire varsity do under 16 seconds. I was amazed by what happened. One player timed at 14.9, a group of players were in there at 15.1 and 15.2, and 9 players total were under 16 seconds. Our legs were weapons. Our opponents found that shots that were winners against other teams came back one more time. We were able to put a tremendous amount of pressure on other teams, by making it very difficult to win a point. We won our miracle title that year. These kids were not physically talented per se, they just worked very hard to use all they had.

In the finals of the boy's singles championship my top player was the #1 seed playing against #2 seed who was very motivated to beat my top player in the finals. My player had won some very closely contested matches, including a come-from-behind three-set win, so we expected a tough match. Since the third setter, my #1 had taken a few more tenths of a second from his spider run time, and had greatly improved his anaerobic endurance. Not only did he cruise to a 6-3, 6-2 win, but twice there were moments where the other player's fans wanted to clap, because they thought he had hit a clear winner. I too was convinced that one particular shot would not be reached. The #1 player reached it, and hit the ball back better, and the fans were stunned they had to stop clapping for the winner that did not happen! That was a truly stunning moment.

CHAPTER SEVENTY-FOUR
The Formula for Success

I interviewed Sean Brawley, one of the most notable success coaches in the U.S. on my radio blog at www.blogtalkradio.com/ 720degreecoaching. You can listen to those podcasts anytime! Sean who is a success coach to CEOs, corporations, and a certain NFL Super Bowl-winning head coach named Pete Carroll spoke at length about his journey and the journeys of some of his clients in reaching for success. Sean helped and work alongside Pete after he was fired by the New England Patriots thinking he may never get another opportunity to be a head coach in the NFL again. Sean helped Pete adjust his coaching philosophy, and gain the head coaching job at USC, and the rest is history. Carroll is now known for being a very innovative coach. Like him or not, NFL players recently were polled and he was the #1 coach for whom they would like to play. Sean shared a formula that you can ponder: Performance = Potential − Interference. The maximum performance of our players will be increased, when we can decrease the amount of interference there is moving toward our objectives. Coaches, it's your job to train your team's potential and improve that, and then to reduce the amount of interference, which may be your own.

CHAPTER SEVENTY-FIVE
Do you Really Want to Get Mad?

I'm not a big fan of coaches who are constantly yelling, and I really despise those that use vulgar language often. On the other hand I excuse my own temper because of my Scotch/Irish family tree. I do believe there is a time and place to be furious for the right reasons with boys teams, but I do not recommend losing your cool with the girls, as they might not take it the same way. I have some very strong guidelines to follow. Also, I have had entire seasons where I did not express anger in a loud way at all.

First, you must decide that what is happening actually is unacceptable, and must be addressed with full force. You get one shot at this. If one really good blow up and anger display does not get their attention, then nothing will. Don't waste your emotional energy trying it a second time two in displaying anger, you could get caught sliding down a slippery slope. Teenagers often bait adults to become angry for their own entertainment, so it must also be on your timing.

Second, be sure to do it in the timing that you choose, and for the length of time that you choose. You must not show anger if you are not completely in control of your anger. If you are not thinking and actively choosing, then you may have an issue of anger that needs to be addressed. Because I so rarely get angry with my teams, and almost never use vulgar language, you can be sure that when I do it delivers full shock value. It is like using the paddles on a heart attack victim, you can use them in one short bout, but you can't use them often.

Third, one good yell early in the season gives the players just enough fear and respect, so they will be more careful about what they do. Fourth and final, you must be angry for reasons that have to do your care about their outcomes, and not for your own, otherwise you are just being selfish. The players will know if you care about them, or if you simply care about yourself. You must express deep caring about the people, the enterprise, and the outcomes for them personally in their lives. Anything less and you just become an angry person.

CHAPTER SEVENTY-SIX
The Player/Coach Relationship Gambit

One group of girls, on a not such a great team were losing heart and began to skip practices for 'academic reasons'. I arrived at practice one day with almost half the team was absent. I asked the captain, "Where are these people who are missing?" "Chemistry lab.", was the answer. I left immediately went to the chemistry lab. When I came the girls were just coming out of the lab, and they had that look that says, "caught!" I approached them and said, "Where have you been? I was worried. Is everything okay? Now that I see what you're doing, I'm thinking about what this does for our player/coach relationship. Where is the communication? I need to know where you are. Today, I planned a practice for my full team, I am here to serve you ladies and help you get better at tennis, but you don't even regard my feelings." I could see that tears were beginning to form in their eyes, then they all apologized and promised never to do that again. As I walked away from that, I applauded my own Academy Award-winning performance because I didn't really mean much of what I said. I did it for them; it was what they needed to hear. They never skipped another practice, soon that team would snap its 71-match league losing streak, that had lasted six full years.

CHAPTER SEVENTY-SEVEN
Captains Out of Control

Just as great captains on a team can help make for a great season, bad captains can make for a horrible one. I'm very happy to report that rarely have I ever had bad team captains. This section could be very long in the telling, but I will give one anecdote. You can decide if these girls fit the mold of the pre-teen terror movie about the nice girl who goes to a private school only to be terrorized by the mean girls. My number one player was a valiant warrior, good player, played hurt, gave of herself, and was positive, friendly, and helpful. The team captains, it turned out, held veiled jealousy of her all season long. This made for some very uncomfortable situations all season long. I had to remove one captain from her role, after an embarrassing outburst in which she threatened a rival with physical harm. The #1 player then stepped into that role.

It all ended in the following way, and it tells all you need to know. At our very poorly planned and executed end of the season "dessert," most of the team met for the conclusion of the season. The captains did not put enough thought into making sure everyone on our very small team could come. Some players stopped by for a moment, others lingered. The captain and one friend left our table to "go get something." I was thinking, "Great they are getting my gift for the season." Instead they came back with ice cream cones filled with whipped cream, with a look on their faces like they were up to something. I was ready to defend myself, and if they had come toward me, whipped cream would have gone everywhere. Instead, one girl lightly dabbed some whipped cream on the cheek of her friend, while the other "oops, I slipped", shoving whipped cream all over the face of our top player. In a move of pure class, the top player gave a courtesy laugh, got up, cleaned up, stayed two more minutes, and then said, "Well, that's enough for me; good night." I was shocked, and my sincere hope is that you never experience working at a school with kids like that. Had I returned for a second year of coaching, I know changing the culture of that team would be a monumental task.

CHAPTER SEVENTY-EIGHT
Magic Cue for Better Performance

My friend Bryden Yemm, taught me something incredible, the power of the phrase, "play better." If your player is playing poorly, advise them to play better, and ask them to repeat, "I want to play better; I can play better; I will play better,"--and they will. Rather than invest energy into self criticism, the players can refocus on that idea and raise their game. Give it a try. It's almost magic.

CHAPTER SEVENTY-NINE
Crosscourt - The Staple, Down the Line - Dessert

Crosscourt - The Staple

I find that many coaches overestimate the maturity of their players, and some of them have grandiose visions of the intricate strategies that their players will execute for them. I am the opposite for two reasons. Two of the very best tactical thinkers in tennis, Greg Patton (no relation, thank goodness) and Allen Fox, both espouse the simplicity of cross-court play. I see many teenagers hit the ball down the line too early in a rally and give away the tactical advantage.

Every day in practice we will have a cross-court rally of some type. Prior to every single match, I remind my players, "Build the point with cross-court shots when you get the short ball, then use your creativity." While everything is equal in a rally, or if your player is experiencing pressure from the other player, it is imperative to defend cross-court almost constantly. Players need to be patient and happy to hit another cross-court. I have seen many examples of two players who are very nearly equal, but one player hit the ball cross-court more often and won in routine fashion. One of the finest books you can read in regard to understanding singles play is *Pressure Tennis* by Paul Wardlaw.

204

There will come a time when you hit a cross-court that is a little better than the others, forcing your opponent into a tough spot and gaining the short ball from them. As for training the understanding of cross court, I like to put a cone in the middle of the quadrant to show neutral and aggressive angles.

I liken the strategy of playing the short ball to playing offense in football. The more and wider area that the other team has to defend, the more they have to think about, and then larger openings are created. If you have a great shot down the line to one corner, being able to hit a nice drop shot to the opposite corner diagonally creates quite a bit of worry for the opponent.

I define an attackable short ball as one where the player can move forward into the court, and comfortably get to the ball on balance. If we take the court and split it into thirds, then we have the outer third to the forehand, the middle third where mostly forehands will be hit, and the final third which is the backhand. In this area of the court, everyone differs somewhat in their comfort level with certain kinds of shots.

Going Down the Line - The Dessert

I like my players to first work on hitting the winner or approach shot down the line. This is the most common and easy way to win a point on the short ball. When hit well, it's either a winner or becomes a strong forcing shot where the player keeps the upper hand in the point. At the very least, you have put the other player out of position. I want my players to be able to hit a corner ball from all three areas. Additionally, we can talk about specific shots that work better in different thirds. Highly skilled players should have at least two options from each third of the court. In the forehand third, the next great shot to hit is the rolling angled topspin shot, the drop shot to the opposite side, or the tricky drop shot straight ahead to fool the player that ran full sprint to cover the other two. Of course, you can also hit a deep cross-court shot, but you run the risk of letting the player back into the point.

From the middle of the court, you have to be a highly skilled player to hit a great angle to the sides, so with 99% of my players I have them go deep to the opposite corner or use the drop shot to the side. Sometimes this is the best position from which to wrong foot the opponent, looking for a weak reply that you can volley, or hit a standard approach shot and come to the net.

The backhand side for some players can limit their creativity, so its best to build in their bread and butter shot. Whether it's the winner, approach or angle to the other side, that's the shot they will hit 80% or more of the time, and attempt the other shots sometimes simply to keep the opponent guessing.

CHAPTER EIGHTY
Strategy as an Expression of Personality

There are five basic strategies for winning a tennis match. From these a player may choose an A game, B game, and if they are quite good, a C game. Seldom does anyone master all five. Here they are in my order of preference. This chapter gave rise to another book that I wrote, _Top 5 Strategies and Tactics for Winning Tennis_ which is a print book and an eBook. In the print book version you also get two bonus books.

1. **Overpower your opponent.** Whenever you have the opportunity to overpower your opponent   and play first strike tennis, you should. This is the best way to win quickly and conserve energy.

2. **Pressure your opponents position.** Use shot combinations to move opponent out of position to "Control, Hurt, Finish." Works great unless the other player is better at it, than you, and/or they are a much better mover on court.

3. **Pressure your opponents time.** Move closer and take away time from your opponent, force them to need a great show now. Come to the net. This is seldom used. Moving closer to take away time is important for a player who may lack foot speed.

4. **Disrupt their rhythm.** Vary your shots, high and low, fast and slow, vary the angles, and the spins. This works great for a full match, but can also be used in a match to wreck the opponent so you can go back to your A game. Caution, your opponent may become angry with themselves or you.

5. **Last of all, the worst strategy for winning a match.** Simply keeping the ball in play and being consistent uses the most energy. This will make all your matches more difficult than if you had used Strategies 1 through 4. You will retire early, and be a poor doubles player. Of course, on the day, this may be the only effective strategy, but please don't make it a lifestyle. I offer game style coaching to help players play in a way that expresses who they are, rather than what they have been told about how people "should" play.

CHAPTER EIGHTY-ONE
Percentage Tennis

Before you do anything with specific game styles there are some very important universal truths of strategy to cover:

* **First serve %** is still the number one statistic in all of tennis. All players at the US Open this year combined won 70% of the points when they got their first serve in.

* Explaining first serve % can be simplified to "If you miss a first serve, then you have to **make the the next two.**", If you want to have 65% first serves in play. Sometimes this is what it takes for some players to understand the impact of the statistic.

* **Attacking second serve** with power, approach shots, angles or drop shots is your best possible chance for a high winning percentage on return games.

* In rallies, the second most effective play among all shots is an approach shot to the backhand, according to Brain Game Tennis guru Craig O'Shanessy. **63% of points were won when approaching the net to the backhand side of the opponent**, either down the line or cross court.

* In high school play, its acceptable to have **up to 2 unforced errors for every winner**, and when you throw in forced errors by the opponent you gain an edge.

* It's **unnacceptable** to have more than a **5:1 ratio of errors to winners**.

* It's much **easier to reduce your errors** with better footwork and shorter backswings than it is to increase your winners without making additional errors.

* It does not really matter how much speed or how much spin the shot has if its not in the court. Teenagers are maybe the most susceptible to wanting to look good, even if the results are not as good.

CHAPTER EIGHTY-TWO
Doubles Strategy Fundamentals

When developing strategy, it's great to remember the teenage mind. It was recently discovered that the brain of a teenager has physical and developmental markers that explain much of their behavior, and guide us adults to know how to help. In a nutshell, the parts of the brain that lead to feelings of danger and alarm become more developed, while the cerebral cortex which regulates these reactions is not fully connected and developed. Teenagers need the steadying hand of a coach.

Why does this relate to strategy? Because of this tendency toward alarm, the incoming ball can create enough fear to render thinking about strategy a much more difficult endeavor. For that reason, I like to keep strategies simple, manageable, and just slightly challenging. As players develop a fundamental strategy, we move into the next level of strategy, building one piece at a time. One of the great aspects of doubles is that each player has a peer that can help remind them of the strategy in place and support the execution. It's also paramount to help players not to be afraid of being at the net.

Basic Doubles Played Well

The server serves from midway between the center line and the singles sideline, but can move slightly to the right if the returner has remarkable angled returns. Serves to the T, serving to the T, instead of out wide, allows the net person to get more winning volleys, makes the down the line return a very low percentage, and reduces the angle by which they return the ball to the server. I work hard to instill in my players the desire to try to hit this 80% of the time.

Body serves comprise another 10 to 15%, and wide serves 5 to 10%. Of course, if you fail to hit the T, you can justify it as "mixing things up." That rationale seems to help those who need more control on their serve. The most important aspects of the serve are depth, placement, spin, and speed. The depth and placement keeps players from teeing off. The spin aids in forcing the returner into a higher return that the net man can pick off. Keep working on your serve until the other teams keep giving your net man high balls.

The server's net man is the most crucial member of the team. They should stand in the exact middle of the service box for starters. If they are close to 5' tall or even shorter, I like to have them stand back as far as one foot in front of the service line. Being sure to reduce the amount of successful lobs is an important part of high school doubles. Also, being in a position that allows you to move diagonally forward for a volley helps it to penetrate the court.

One great thing about short people, is they can hit overheads when taller people would hit a high volley. Shorter players should practice overheads as much as volleys. The servers net man should be ready to move their feet all the way to the center line and be ready to reach across to pick off balls coming across the middle.

Note: This is not poaching. Poaching and switching occurs when the net man's foot crosses the center line. They then should cover that side and partner switches. The most important thing for the net man to do is cover their entire side of the court and reach across a bit to be scary to the other team.

CHAPTER EIGHTY-THREE
Specific Roles in Doubles Positions

Serve Returner

If the serve returner can do two things, they will be highly effective doubles teammates. First, if they can make a short cross-court return within 5 feet of the side T, the net man will almost never touch the ball except in the case of a planned poach, leaving early. Second, if they can lob over the net man to the baseline, they can wreck things for the serving team. All the serving teams plans fall apart when the net man gets lobbed. Mentally, its very important to say, "lob to the baseline", as sometimes players lob the net man, but it goes right in their overhead strike zone. I am in favor of trying to hit to the alley once or twice a set, or a bit more if the net man is very active. This works to keep them honest more than as an attempt to win with low percentage shots. Alley shots at best are a 50/50 proposition, and many times much worse. The primary objective of the service return is to neutralize the net person.

Returners Partner

Subtle position changes by the returner's partner can help you win 5 to 10% more points, which can change a match from a loss to a win. The mistake the returner's partner makes most commonly is staying where they are after the return has been hit. I teach those in this position, that as soon as they are sure the ball is going past the server's net person they should move forward in the court. If there is any doubt that the ball will get through or over the servers partner, they should take at least one or two very quick steps backward to improve the chances of defending by up to 20%.

Moving back even one step, can create more time to see the ball, and give less space for the server's net man to hit into between the two players on this side. If the returner lobs, don't get too close. If the returner has hit a very wide return cross-court, guard your alley. Coaches can see and make adjustments based on how your doubles team plays. The axiom I play by is, "If the net person looks like they may touch it, move back and stop before they hit. As soon as you know the ball will pass the net man, move forward into the service box."

The Server's Net Person

This player needs to be as aggressive as they possibly can to attack the largest possible space at net, especially on the first ball. Much of what is contained in the drills section of this book is meant to support exactly that. This player should be encouraged to be so aggressive that they should be supported and encouraged even if they make a mistake in a serve game. If they were to make two mistakes in the same game, then they can be allowed to be non-aggressive for the remainder of that game.

The Server

The servers job is very simple. They need to put the ball into the box as deep as possible, and if they have a topspin serve, they can make the highest bouncing serve they can. The object is to cause the returner to give the ball back high enough over the net, that it makes for an attackable ball for their net man. When the server does their job, doubles begins to look like volleyball. The server forces the returner to bump the ball up to the net person who then makes the spike or kill. Great doubles teams will have a point or two per game where the net person finishes on the first volley.

CHAPTER EIGHTY-FOUR
Multicultural Tennis

Having spent much of my most formative years living in one of the most integrated cities in America, Oakland in California, I have always had a passion for creating a multicultural team. Over the years, my idealism began to wane, as I saw within my own teams a resistance toward integration. At the very outset of my tennis coaching career, I met one of my closest tennis friends. Mark Manning called me one day to invite my team to a tournament that he was helping to coordinate, that would bring together 32 top teams from 4 different regions around the greater San Francisco Bay Area. Each flight of 8 teams would produce a champion which would play at Stanford University for a grand championship. It was called the Mercedes-Benz Cup. Mark's invitation however was that my team would be an alternate. When his own team from East Oakland had multiple players with ineligibility issues, my team was entered into the event. This started a 23 year friendship that ended in 2012 with the passing of my dear friend.

Mark later ascended to become the first ever African-American USTA Section President, and soon after more were to follow. I want to take this moment not only to honor my dearly departed friend, but also to say I finally reached a level of satisfaction.

Some believe in the law of attraction and I certainly do, but this attraction took many years to find it's fulfillment. This spring I interviewed Angel Lopez a great tennis coach in the San Diego area who was himself coached by Pancho Segura, and we spoke about how we can get more Latino youth playing tennis. Almost casually he mentioned that it can start in the schools. This fall, when I took on a new high school team, much to my surprise our #1 player was a very pleasant Latina. She then inspired not only a number of brand new Latina players to join the girl's team, but also then a group of Latino boy's are planning to come out to for the boy's season in the spring. The great thing that happened is that even though the make up of the team changed dramatically, the unity of the team remained consistent and improved.

Girls with different racial backgrounds were surprised to make new friends that they might not have met before. The leadership group of the team also changed in order to truly represent the make up of the team. Teams have a way of bringing together players from different social sets, to create something bigger and better than what each culture could accomplish separately. Those of you that coach in more polarized areas of the country, I can only hope that you will take on the mantel to open up opportunities to those who historically have not played the game in your area. Open the door!

CHAPTER EIGHTY-FIVE
Culture and Attitudes

Those that know me well will agree that I am uniquely qualified to discuss culture as it relates to teams. Having written a thesis in the area of Cross Cultural Education as a Master's candidate, I spend a considerable amount of time doing focused research on the issues surrounding culture and education. Every culture brings some wonderful strengths to the society to which it belongs. Enjoy those facets of warm and loving behavior, high achievement orientation, fun and playful demeanor. However, the rest of this chapter is going to focus on the negative impacts that different cultures bring to bear. Certainly, there are ways in which culture may infringe on the team atmosphere. Without going into specifics and identifying groups, which on the face of it would be rude, I want to outline some problems that certain cultural traits bring to a unified team setting. Here is a list of bullet points of issues.

Some Cultures May:
* Put the wants and desires of the player ahead of the team.
* Be dishonest, so as to save face.
* Fail to communicate bad news out of shame.
* Suddenly require their child to be home with family.
* Allow for disruptive behavior, even when structured time is required by the coach.

* See their child as being 'the special one', deserving of most attention.
* Not value the team experience, because sport is only a play time to that family.
* Place an academic enrichment in a schedule conflict with a team activity.
* Believe only their child in all they say, even when an adult is informing them of a discrepancy
* Encourage disrespectful behavior in the name of honesty.
* Not aware of the whereabouts of their child.
* Physical or emotional abuse of the student as a matter of course.
* Second guess the coach.
* Be watchful, critical and untrusting of the coach.
* Focused on outcomes, winning and losing.
* Focused only on their child's experience on the team.
* Avoid association with mainstream culture of success.

CHAPTER EIGHTY-SIX
Psychological Cues - The Power of "I Can"

After attending a convention featuring Dr. Gary Sailes, a sport psychologist and professor at the University of Indiana, I came away with a great nugget of wisdom that I shared with my team. He gave presentation about a person's Cognitive Affective Profile. His talk focused on the words we use and how they reflect a way of thinking. Our thoughts in turn, can affect our bodies. This was a core talk from a psychological perspective on the mind/body connection. He did an experiment where he showed an athlete who exhibited more strength and competence while saying, "I can," and conversely weaker and less competent while saying, "I can't." I had heard about the power of saying "I can do it", but it seemed to me simply to be corny positive thinking. My mind would soon change forever on this topic.

At the time I was coaching a team that I thought had enough talent to finish fourth in our nine-team league, but if we pulled a good upset, we might finish third. Upon returning to the team, I expressed to them this idea. "We can win the league championship. Let's do it." I remember it as an inspired moment with all the players getting swept up in excitement. Later, my assistant told me, I was the only one who was excited, and everyone else just took it as more of a matter of fact assertion that, we can do it.

Regardless of the perception of the moment, a funny thing happened. I noticed a very big improvement in the effort level at practice. What had been a hard-working team, became an extremely hard-working team. The level of intensity the players brought to practice, and the hopefulness of what we could do increase dramatically. We were able to improve so much in fundamental play and using high percentage tactics, we were able to make up for our relative lack of talent. Most of the boy's on our team were under 5' 8" and only one had what you would call 'weapons' with his serve and forehand. We also worked very hard to become the fastest team on the court, and our spider run times approached world class. Other teams found it very hard to hit a winner against our players.

We played smart and the team learned how to defeat more talented opponents on a weekly basis. We won four 4-3 matches during the season, and losing two 4-3 matches, but only to the first place team. We were amazed as the first place team lost to the third and fifth place teams to give us a share of the league title. That other team gained the post-season spot, but we also have a banner hanging in the gym as co-champions as a testament to the phrase "We can do it!" I will never forget that in our final 4-3 win, Noli and Manuel were down 5-0 in the third set of a pivotal match, and came back to win that third set 7-5, preserving victory at 4-3 and a share of the league title. Had they not come back from a seemingly impossible margin, no banner in the gym. But... they did it!

CHAPTER EIGHTY-SEVEN
Technology

The use of technology in tennis lags behind many other sports, mainly because of the volume of work that needs to be done to fairly share the time. It's better not to be fair, then it is to leave technology out of your program.

Paper and pencil are still technology. If you are interested in the best possible match charting technology check out Nate Gross's Match Chart Logs on Amazon, these have the subtlety that will be appreciated by top high school players who are vying for sectional and state titles. Some training is needed, but this is a powerful tool. I like paper and pencil, because you can erase, or skip a box. Most apps that you can find for a smartphone have problems in that you can't easily back information out of the program, or they force you to come up with data that you missed, because they are tied to the scoring system.

Another way to chart is simply to use some graph paper, in 4 lines you can record a few stats. Lets say you are playing no-ad. Then you need a 4 x 7 grid to allow for capturing the total possible 7 points. On the top line you record if the server made their first serve by writing a 1, or second serve with a 2, or D for double fault. On the second line, you can record if your player hit the final shot, on the third line you can record the opponent. With the majority of high school tennis players, if you simply record whether the shot was a winner W with a circle, was in the net N, long L or wide W, you can start to see which is your player's and opponent's most common error.   Eliminate or reduce your most common error, then watch your results get better!

It seems everyone these days has the ability to film players at 120 to 240 FPS meaning you can watch players in slow motion. Be sure to get permission from the school to do such filming and expect NOT to be able to share that video anywhere.

CHAPTER EIGHTY-EIGHT
Celebrate Often

No matter what happens with your team, whether or not you had a great season or a difficult one, it's time to celebrate. Celebrate that it's over! For adults 10 to 12 weeks seems like a blink of an eye, but to teenagers, it can feel like an eternity. At school banquets, I am the coach who takes the full time addressing my players and honoring them, much to the chagrin of other teams.

So take your time, think about each player, find something positive to say about each one, and express a vision for what they can become. How well you end the season and show gratitude to everyone who helped and worked so hard, helps set a tone for the following year. Consider carefully how awards are given, is the process fair? Are the award appropriate? Does your team want to have other awards like "craziest hair," "funniest player," or "best team player." Make up your own categories. I have had "player of the month" awards, where the winner gets a toy from a kids meal at a fast food place. Believe it or not, teenage boys will fight over that. The final "player of the month" award, is the unofficial "player of the year." It's not an MVP award, it's the one player who made the biggest difference to his or her teammates or coach. I had a player from Czech Republic who came as an exchange student, played on the team, received the final "player of the month" award, and when he received the toy, he cried.

Another thing you can do that is very powerful is get a small item that has lasting value, but does not cost an arm and leg. I have bought a few keychain items, and would give them as a "career achievement award." Its almost 20 years later, and I still have the one I gave myself. Periodically award a player who has had a distinguished four-year career and made a tremendous difference on the direction of the program. In the six years I was at one school, I gave four awards of that type--two to league champions, two to culture changing players.

Enjoy your season, respond to this book, and here is to your better and greater success as you move forward applying what you have learned. I welcome any feedback, and if you have a contribution for me for inclusion, I will consider it, and if I include it, then you will receive some free copies of the new addition of the print book when it becomes available. This book will be updated periodically!

Enjoy your team, have a plan, make it fun, and believe in their best!

About the Author Bill Patton started coaching tennis in 1988, and has 26 seasons of combined coaching experience with boys and girls teams. He is a certified USPTA Elite, PTR Professional, and MTM Professional. Bill now has authored 11 books, and published a fiction title. In a three season span, one of his teams swept the Team, Individual Singles and Doubles titles, setting a record for most participants in sectional individual play. During those three seasons, those teams also defeated two #2 seeds, and two #1 seeds in playoff action. At another school his teams won the only two league titles in a 44-year span for school. In Bill's first year with a perennial last place team, the boys stopped their 37-match league losing streak, while the girls stopped their 71-match streak and were featured on local TV. In 2015 one of his players won the first ever tennis title of any kind in the school's 60 year history. Bill and Styrling Strother his close friend are launching USATennisCoach in December 2015 - usatenniscoach.com

Free Offer: When you buy The Art of Coaching High School Tennis in paperback,

email bill@pattonschooloftennis.com for your choice of free eBook from among his other titles.

If you own the first edition of this book, take a picture of it, send it to Bill for 25% off the new book and he will autographed for you.

Check Out Our Friends!

Craig O'Shanessy BrainGameTennis.com

Be Original, Be Bones! Rocking Team Tennis Uniforms

www.bonesoriginalusa.com

Hyper Optimized Practice Learning Utility

hoplu.com   High School Package Special

*Free Skype walk through and tool education session with coach/ founder Alex.

*Reduced special pricing options.

The coaching tool that supercharges individual development through support team collaboration to produce real results. Supercharge your team with hoplu by contacting alex@hoplu.com today! (reference this book for the offer)

Bill Patton's Amazon Author Page

http://amzn.to/1K6DTxm

720 Degree Tennis Radio Blog

http://www.blogtalkradio.com/720degreecoaching (click follow)

USATennisCoach usatenniscoach.com (coming soon)

43788268R00132

Made in the USA
San Bernardino, CA
27 December 2016